English Grammar for Students of French

The Study Guide
for Those Learning French

Sixth edition

Jacqueline Morton

*with the collaboration of **Helene Neu**,*
The University of Michigan, Ann Arbor

The Olivia and Hill Press®

THE O&H STUDY GUIDES
Jacqueline Morton, editor

English Grammar for Students of Spanish
English Grammar for Students of French
English Grammar for Students of German
English Grammar for Students of Italian
English Grammar for Students of Latin
English Grammar for Students of Russian
English Grammar for Students of Japanese
English Grammar for Students of Arabic
English Grammar for Students of Chinese
Gramática española para estudiantes de inglés

© 2009, Jacqueline Morton

Printed in the U.S.A.

ISBN: 978-0-934034-37-1

Library of Congress Control Number: 2007941964

CONTENTS

Study Tips	1
Study guide	1
Tips for learning vocabulary	1
Tips for learning word forms	3
List of Study Tips	4
1. What's in a Word?	5
2. What is a Noun?	8
3. What is Meant by Gender?	10
4. What is Meant by Number?	13
5. What is an Article?	15
Definite articles	15
Indefinite articles	17
Partitive articles	18
Study Tips — Nouns and their gender	20
6. What is the Possessive?	21
7. What is a Verb?	23
8. What is the Infinitive?	25
Consulting the dictionary	26
Study Tips — Verbs	27
9. What is a Subject?	28
10. What is a Pronoun?	30
11. What is a Subject Pronoun?	32
Study Tips — Subject pronouns	36
12. What is a Verb Conjugation?	37
Choosing the proper "person"	38
How to conjugate a verb	41
Study Tips — Verb conjugations	42
13. What are Auxiliary Verbs?	44
14. What are Affirmative and Negative Sentences?	47
Negative Words	48
15. What are Declarative and Interrogative Sentences?	50
Tag questions	51
16. What is Meant by Tense?	53
Study Tips — Tenses	54
17. What is the Present Tense?	56
18. What is a Participle?	58
Present participle	58
Past participle	59
19. What is the Past Tense?	61
Le passé composé (present perfect)	61
L'imparfait (imperfect)	63
Selection: **le passé composé** or **l'imparfait**	64
Study Tips — The **passé composé**	65

CONTENTS

20. What is the Past Perfect Tense?   67
21. What is the Future Tense?   70
    The immediate future   71
    Study Tips — The future tense   72
22. What is the Future Perfect Tense?   73
23. What is Meant by Mood?   75
24. What is the Imperative?   77
25. What is the Conditional?   79
    Present conditional   79
    Past conditional   80
    If-clauses sequence of tenses   81
    Use of the conditional in indirect speech   82
26. What is the Subjunctive?   83
27. What is an Adjective?   85
28. What is a Descriptive Adjective?   86
    Attributive and predicate Adjectives   87
    Study Tips — Descriptive adjectives   88
29. What is Meant by Comparison of Adjectives?   89
    Comparative   89
    Superlative   90
30. What is a Possessive Adjective?   92
    Singular possessor: *my, your, his, her, its*   93
    Plural possessor: *our, your, their*   94
    Study Tips — Possessive adjectives   96
31. What is an Interrogative Adjective?   97
32. What is a Demonstrative Adjective?   99
33. What is an Adverb?   101
    Adverb or adjective?   102
    Study Tips — Adverbs   103
34. What is a Conjunction?   104
    Study Tips — Conjunctions and the subjunctive   105
35. What is a Preposition?   106
    Study Tips — Prepositions   107
36. What are Objects?   109
    Direct object   109
    Indirect object   110
    Sentences with a direct and an indirect object   111
    Object of a preposition   112
    Relationship of a verb to its object   112

CONTENTS

37. What is an Object Pronoun? 115
    French direct object pronouns 116
    French indirect object pronouns 118
    Summary of object pronouns 120
    Study Tips — Object pronouns 122
38. What is a Disjunctive Pronoun? 123
    French pronouns as objects of a preposition 124
    Summary of object and disjunctive pronouns 127
39. What are Reflexive Pronouns and Verbs? 129
    Reciprocal action 131
40. What is a Possessive Pronoun? 133
    Singular possessor: *mine, yours, his, hers* 134
    Plural possessor: *ours, yours, theirs* 136
    Study Tips — Possessive pronouns 137
41. What is an Interrogative Pronoun? 139
    Subject 139
    Direct object 140
    Indirect object and object of a preposition 141
    "Which (one), which (ones)" 144
    Study Tips — Interrogative pronouns 146
42. What is a Relative Pronoun? 147
    Subject 148
    Direct object 150
    Indirect object and object of a preposition 151
    French relative pronouns objects of
        prepositions other than **de** 153
    French relative pronouns objects of
        the preposition **de** 154
    Possessive modifier *"whose"* 155
    Relative pronouns without antecedents 157
43. What is a Demonstrative Pronoun? 160
    "This one, that one" and *"these, those"* 160
    To show possession: **celui de** 161
    "The one that": **celui qui, celui que** 163
44. What is Meant by Active and Passive Voice? 165
    Making an active sentence passive 167
    Avoiding the passive voice in French 168
Index 171

STUDY TIPS

English Grammar for Students of French explains the grammatical terms that are in your French textbook and shows you how they relate to English grammar. Once you understand the terms and concepts as they apply to your own language, it will be easier for you to understand what is being introduced in your textbook and by your teacher. To help you become a more efficient language learner, we offer specific Study Tips for learning different types of words.

STUDY GUIDE

Before doing an assignment — Read the sections in *English Grammar* that cover the topics you are going to study in your textbook.

Homework — Take notes as you study your textbook. Highlighting is not sufficient. The more often you write down and use vocabulary and rules, the easier it will be for you to remember them. Oral activities should be done over several short periods of time rather than in one long session.

Written exercises — As you write French words or sentences say them out loud. Each time you write, read, say and hear a word, it reinforces it in your memory.

In class — Take notes. You will know what the teacher considers important and it will reinforce what you are studying.

Objective — You have learned something successfully when you are able to take a blank sheet of paper and write a short sentence in French using the correct form of the French words without reference to a textbook or dictionary. The Study Tips below and throughout this handbook will help you with this learning process.

TIPS FOR LEARNING VOCABULARY

One aspect of language learning is remembering a number of foreign words.

To learn vocabulary — Flashcards are a good, handy tool for learning new words and their meaning. You can carry them with you, group them as you wish and add information as you advance. Creating your own flashcards is an important first step in learning vocabulary.

1. Write the French word or expression on one side of an index card and its English equivalent on the other side.

2. On the French side add a short sentence using the word or expression. To make sure that your sentence is grammatically correct, copy an example from your textbook substituting the names of people and places with ones you know. It will make it easier for you to remember a word in a familiar context. For review purposes, note down the chapter and page number of your textbook where the word is introduced.

3. On the French side include any irregularities and whatever information is relevant to the word in question. You will find specific suggestions under the Study Tips sections of this handbook.

How to use the cards — Regardless of the side you're working on, always say the French word out loud.

1. Look at the French side first. Going from French to English is easier than from English to French because it only requires your recognizing the French word. Read the French word(s) out loud, giving the English equivalent, then check your answer on the English side.

2. When you go easily from French to English, turn the cards to the English side. Going from English to French is harder than going from French to English because you have to pull the word and its spelling out of your memory. Say the French equivalent out loud as you write it down, then check the spelling. Some students prefer closing their eyes and visualizing the French word and its spelling.

3. As you progress, put aside the cards you know and concentrate on the ones you still don't know.

How to remember words — Below are suggestions to help you associate a French word with an English word with a similar meaning. This is the first step and it will put the French word in your short-term memory. Use and practice, the next step, will put the words in your long-term memory.

1. There are many words, called COGNATES, that have the same meaning and approximately the same spelling in English as in French. These words are easy to recognize in French, but you will have to concentrate on the differences in spelling and pronunciation.

English	French
activity	activité
music	musique
furious	furieux

2. Try to associate the French word with an English word that has a related meaning.

French	English	Related English word
l'avion	*the plane*	aviation
beau	*handsome*	beauty
le vent	*the wind*	ventilation

90

3. If the French word has no similarities to English, rely on any association that is meaningful to you. The more associations you have for a word, i.e., the more "hooks," the easier it will be for you to remember it. Different types of associations work for different people. Find the one that works best for you. Here are some suggestions:

- Group words by topics or personal associations — It is easier to learn new words if you group them. You can group them according to topics such as food, clothing, activities you do for fun, sports, school, home, or according to personal associations such as things you carry in your backpack, things you'd take on a desert island, gifts you'd like to receive, etc.

100

- Associate the word with an image — If you have trouble remembering a particular word, you might want to create a "bizarre image" in your mind with which to associate it. This method is very subjective and only works for some people.

110

  la maison = *house*
  "She goes to the *house* in **May** with her **son**."

  l'eau = *water*
  "I jumped into the cold *water* and shouted: "oh, oh!!""

4. To reinforce the French word and its spelling, use it in a short sentence.

TIPS FOR LEARNING WORD FORMS

Another aspect of language learning is remembering the various forms a word can take; for example, another form of *book* is *books* and *do* can take the form of *does* and *did*. As a general rule, the first part of the word indicates its meaning and the second part indicates its form.

120

To learn forms — Paper and pencil are the best tools to learn the various forms of a word. You can write them down until you get them right. The following steps will make learning forms easier.

1. Look for a pattern in the different forms of a word.
   - Which letters, if any, remain constant?
   - Which letters change?
   - Is there a pattern to the changes?
   - Is this pattern the same as one you already know?
   - If this pattern is similar to one you already know, what are the similarities and differences?

   We will help you establish patterns in the Study Tips following selected chapters.

2. Once you have established the pattern, it will be easy to memorize the forms.
   - Take a blank piece of paper and write down the forms while saying them out loud.
   - Continue until you are able to write all the forms correctly without referring to your textbook.

3. Write short sentences using the various forms.

To review forms — You can use flashcards to review forms. You will find suggestions on what to write on the cards under Study Tips.

LIST OF STUDY TIPS

Nouns and their gender	20
Verbs	27
Subject pronouns	36
Verb conjugations	42
Tenses	54
The **passé composé**	65
The future tense	72
Descriptive adjectives	88
Possessive adjectives	96
Adverbs	103
Conjunctions and the subjunctive	105
Prepositions	107
Object pronouns	122
Possessive pronouns	137
Interrogative pronouns	146

WHAT'S IN A WORD?

When you learn a foreign language, in this case French, you must look at each word in four ways: MEANING, PART OF SPEECH, FUNCTION and FORM.

MEANING

An English word may be connected to a French word that has a similar meaning.

> *Boy*, a young male child, has the same meaning as the French word **garçon**.

Words with equivalent meanings are learned by memo- rizing VOCABULARY (see pp. 1-4).

In addition, every language has expressions that can't be translated word-for-word. These are called IDIOMATIC EXPRESSIONS, or IDIOMS. For instance, the French equivalent of *"to be* hungry" and *"to be* thirsty" are "**avoir** faim" and "**avoir** soif" [word-for-word: *to have* hunger, *to have* thirst]. Similarly, the English expression *"to take* a walk" is "**faire** une promenade" [word-for-word: *to make* a walk]. You will have to be on the alert for these idioms because a word-for-word translation from one language to another would be meaningless.

PART OF SPEECH

In English and French words are grouped according to how they are used in a sentence. There are eight groups corresponding to eight PARTS OF SPEECH:

nouns	articles
verbs	adverbs
pronouns	prepositions
adjectives	conjunctions

Some parts of speech are further broken down according to type. Adjectives, for instance, can be descriptive, interrogative, demonstrative, or possessive. Each part of speech has its own rules for spelling, pronunciation, and use.

You will have to identify an English word's part of speech in order to choose the correct French equivalent. For example, look at the word *plays* in the following two sentences. In each sentence it belongs to a different part of speech, each one corresponding to a different French word.

John *plays* squash.

verb → **joue**

John likes *plays*.

noun → **pièces**

The various sections of this handbook show you how to identify parts of speech so that you are able to choose the proper French words and the rules that apply to them.

FUNCTION

In English and French the role a word plays in a sentence is called its FUNCTION. For example, words that are nouns can have the following functions:

> subject
> direct object
> indirect object
> object of a preposition

You will have to identify an English word's function in order to choose the correct French equivalent. For example, look at the word *him* in the following two sentences. In each sentence it has a different function, each one corresponding to a different French word.

John sees *him*.

direct object → **le**

John gives *him* the book.

indirect object → **lui**

The various sections of this handbook show you how to identify the function of words in English and in French so that you can to choose the proper French words and the rules that apply to them.

FORM

In English and in French, a word can influence the form of another word, that is, its spelling and pronunciation. This "matching" is called AGREEMENT and it is said that one word "agrees" with another.

I am	*am* agrees with *I*
she is	*is* agrees with *she*

Agreement does not play a big role in English, but it is an important part of the French language. For example, look at the sentences below where the lines indicate which words must agree with one another.

*The beautiful white **car** belongs to my big brother.*

La belle **voiture** blanche appartient à mon grand **frère**.

In English, the only word that affects another word in the sentence is *car*, which forces us to say *belongs*. If we changed *car* to *cars*, we would have to say *belong* to make it agree with *cars*.

In French, the word for *car* (**voiture**) affects the word for *belongs* (**appartient**), as well as the French words for *the* (**la**), *beautiful* (**belle**) and *white* (**blanche**). The word for *brother* (**frère**) affects the French words for *my* (**mon**) and *big* (**grand**). If we changed *car* to *cars* and *brother* to *brothers* all the affected words would also have to be changed.

As the various parts of speech are introduced in this handbook, we will go over "agreement" so that you learn which words agree with others and how the agreement is shown.

8

2

WHAT IS A NOUN?

A **NOUN** is a word that can be the name of a person, animal, place, thing, event or idea.

▪ a person	professor, clown, student, girl
	Professor Smith, Bozo, Paul, Mary
▪ an animal	dog, bird, bear, snake
	Heidi, Tweetie, Teddy
▪ a place	city, state, country, continent
	stadium, restaurant, France, Europe
▪ a thing	lamp, airplane, book, dress
	Perrier, Eiffel Tower, Arch of Triumph
▪ an event or activity	graduation, marriage, birth, death
	football, robbery, rest, growth
▪ an idea or concept	poverty, democracy, humor, mathematics
	addition, strength, elegance, virtue

As you can see, a noun is not only a word which names something that is tangible (i.e., that you can touch), such as *table, dog,* and *White House,* it can also be the name of things that are abstract (i.e., that you cannot touch), such as *justice, jealousy,* and *honor.*

A noun that does not state the name of a specific person, place, thing, etc. is called a **COMMON NOUN.** A common noun does not begin with a capital letter, unless it is the first word of a sentence. All the words above that are not capitalized are common nouns.

A noun that is the name of a specific person, place, thing, etc. is called a **PROPER NOUN.** A proper noun always begins with a capital letter. All the words above that are capitalized are proper nouns.

Mary is a girl.
proper common
noun   noun

A noun that is made up of two words is called a **COMPOUND NOUN.** A compound noun can be composed of two common nouns, such as *comic strip* and *ice cream* or two proper nouns, such as *North America.*

IN ENGLISH

To help you learn to recognize nouns, look at the paragraph below where the nouns are in *italics*.

> The best *products* from *France* include *wines, perfumes, scarves, gloves* and other luxury *items*. Today, French *workers* make excellent *skis* and *tennis rackets* that are sold the *world* over. Thanks to the *European Union*, you can find *goods* from *Germany, Italy, England,* and their commercial *partners* in all large French *stores*. Thus, Italian *sports car*s, English *leather*, German *glassware*, and Belgian *lace* can be bought at *prices* comparable to those in the *country* of *origin*.

IN FRENCH

Nouns are identified in the same way as they are in English.

TERMS USED TO TALK ABOUT NOUNS

- **GENDER** — In French a noun has a gender; that is, it can be classified according to whether it is masculine or feminine (see *What is Meant by Gender?*, p. 10).

- **NUMBER** — A noun has a number; that is, it can be identified according to whether it is singular or plural (see *What is Meant by Number?*, p. 13).

- **COUNT** OR **NON-COUNT** — A noun can be classified as to whether it is a count noun or non-count noun; that is, whether it refers to something that can be counted or not (see p. 19 in *What is an Article?*).

- **FUNCTION** — A noun can have a variety of functions in a sentence; that is, it can be the subject of the sentence (see *What is a Subject?*, p. 28) or an object (see *What are Objects?*, p. 109).

STUDY TIPS — NOUNS AND THEIR GENDER (SEE P. 20)

CHAPTER

3

WHAT IS MEANT BY GENDER?

GENDER in the grammatical sense means that a word can be classified as masculine, feminine, or neuter.

> Did Paul give Mary the book?
> Yes, *he* gave *it* to *her*.
> | | |
>   masc. neuter fem.

Gender is not very important in English; however, it is at the very heart of the French language where the gender of a word is often reflected not only in the way the word itself is spelled and pronounced, but also in the way all the words connected to it are spelled and pronounced.

More parts of speech have a gender in French than in English.

ENGLISH	FRENCH
pronouns	nouns
possessive adjectives	articles
	pronouns
	adjectives

Since each part of speech follows its own rules to indicate gender, you will find gender discussed in the chapters dealing with articles and the various types of pronouns and adjectives. In this section we shall only look at the gender of nouns.

IN ENGLISH

Nouns themselves do not have a gender, but sometimes their meaning indicates a gender based on the biological sex of the person or animal the noun stands for. For instance, when we replace a proper or common noun that refers to a man or a woman, we use *he* for males and *she* for females.

- nouns referring to males indicate the MASCULINE gender

   Paul came home; *he* was tired, and I was glad to see *him*.
    | | |
  noun (male)   masculine   masculine

- nouns referring to females indicate the FEMININE gender

   Mary came home; *she* was tired, and I was glad to see *her*.
    | | |
  noun (female) feminine   feminine

All the proper or common nouns that do not have a bio-logical gender are considered **NEUTER** and are replaced by *it*.

The city of Washington is lovely. I enjoyed visiting *it*.
        | |
    noun   neuter

IN FRENCH

All nouns — common nouns and proper nouns — have a gender; they are either masculine or feminine. Do not confuse the grammatical terms "masculine" and "feminine" with the terms "male" and "female." Only a few French nouns have a grammatical gender tied to whether they refer to someone of the male or female sex; most nouns have a gender that must be memorized.

The gender of common and proper nouns based on **BIOLOGICAL GENDER** is easy to determine. These are nouns whose meaning can only refer to one or the other of the biological sexes, male or female.

MALES → MASCULINE	FEMALES → FEMININE
Paul	Mary
boy	girl
brother	sister
son	daughter

The gender of most nouns, common and proper, cannot be explained or figured out. These nouns only have a **GRAMMATICAL GENDER** that is unrelated to biological sex and that must be memorized. Here are some examples of English nouns classified under the gender of their French equivalent.

MASCULINE	FEMININE
boat	car
suicide	death
Japan	France
blackboard	chalk
government	democracy

Textbooks and dictionaries usually indicate the gender of a noun with an *m.* for masculine or an *f.* for feminine. Sometimes the indefinite articles are used: *un* for masculine or *une* for feminine (see *What is an Article?*, p. 15). As you learn a new noun always learn its gender because it will affect the spelling and pronunciation of the words related to it.

Here is a list of some noun endings that often, but not always, indicate a noun's gender:

MASCULINE

-age	avantage, garage, bagage
-eau	chapeau *(hat)*, manteau *(coat)*, cadeau *(gift)*
-et	objet, sujet, secret
-isme	capitalisme, impressionnisme, tourisme
-ment	gouvernement, monument, événement *(event)*
-oir	miroir *(mirror)*, soir *(evening)*, couloir *(hallway)*

FEMININE

-ace/	glace *(ice cream)*, place, surface
-asse	impasse *(cul-de-sac)*, classe
-aison	maison *(house)*, saison *(season)*, comparaison
-ance/	tolérance, assurance *(insurance)*, substance
-ence	présence, absence, compétence
-ade	promenade *(walk)*, escapade, ambassade
-esse	promesse *(promise)*, adresse, richesse
-ette	cassette, bicyclette, serviette *(napkin)*
-ière	lumière *(light)*, bière *(beer)*, manière *(manner)*
-sion/	télévision, décision, profession, compréhension
-tion	nation, production, compétition
-té	société, liberté, nationalité, beauté *(beauty)*
-tude	étude *(study)*, attitude, solitude
-ure	ceinture *(belt)*, aventure, nature, peinture *(painting)*

CAREFUL — Do not rely on noun endings to determine a noun's grammatical gender as there are many exceptions. Always check the gender in your textbook or the dictionary. Also, do not rely on biological gender to indicate the grammatical gender of French nouns that can refer to a man or a woman. For instance, the grammatical gender of the noun **personne** *(person)* is always feminine, even though it can refer to a man or woman.

STUDY TIPS — NOUNS AND THEIR GENDER (SEE P. 20)

WHAT IS MEANT BY NUMBER?

NUMBER in the grammatical sense means that a word can be
classified as singular or plural. When a word refers to one
person or thing, it is said to be **SINGULAR**; when it refers to
more than one, it is **PLURAL**.

one *book*   two *books*
| |
singular   plural

More parts of speech indicate number in French than in
English and there are more spelling and pronunciation
changes in French than in English.

ENGLISH	FRENCH
nouns	nouns
verbs	verbs
pronouns	pronouns
demonstrative adjectives	adjectives
	articles

Since each part of speech follows its own rules to indicate
number, you will find number discussed in the chapters
dealing with articles, the various types of adjectives and pronouns, as well as in all the sections on verbs. In this section
we shall only look at the number of nouns.

IN ENGLISH

A singular noun is made plural in one of two ways:

1. some singular nouns add an *"-s"* or *"-es"*

book   books
kiss   kisses

2. other singular nouns change their spelling

man   men
mouse   mice
leaf   leaves
child   children

Some nouns, called **COLLECTIVE NOUNS**, refer to a group of persons or things, but the noun itself is considered singular.

The *team* has eleven players.
The *family* is well.

IN FRENCH

As in English, the plural form of a noun is usually spelled differently from the singular.

The most common change is the same as the one made in English; that is, an "**-s**" is added to the singular masculine or feminine noun.

	SINGULAR	PLURAL		
MASCULINE	livre	livres	*book*	*books*
FEMININE	table	tables	*table*	*tables*

Some nouns indicate the plural differently. When that is the case, your textbook will give you the plural form.

As in English, French collective nouns are considered singular.

> **L'équipe a** onze joueurs.
> *The team has eleven players.*
> |
> singular

> **La famille va** bien.
> *The family is well.*
> |
> singular

HEARING THE PLURAL

In English you can always hear the plural in the noun itself.

SINGULAR	PLURAL
the *book*	the *books*
the *dress*	the *dresses*
the *child*	the *child**ren***

In French, even though you can usually see the plural ending of the noun, you don't hear it in the noun itself because the final "s" is not pronounced.

same pronunciation

livre	livres
robe	robes
enfant	enfants

To know whether a noun is singular or plural, you will have to listen to the words before the noun, such as **le, la, l'** for the singular or **les** for the plural (see *What is an Article*, p. 15).

SINGULAR	PLURAL
le livre	**les** livres
la robe	**les** robes
l'enfant	**les** enfants

5

WHAT IS AN ARTICLE?

An ARTICLE is a word placed before a noun to show whether   1
the noun refers to a specific person, animal, place, thing,
event or idea, or whether it refers to a non-specific person,
thing, or idea.

> I saw *the* boy you spoke about.
> |
> a specific boy
>
> I saw *a* boy in the street.
> |
> not a specific boy   10

In English and French there are two types of articles, DEFI-
NITE ARTICLES and INDEFINITE ARTICLES.

DEFINITE ARTICLES
IN ENGLISH

A DEFINITE ARTICLE is used before a noun when we are
speaking about a specific person, place, animal, thing, or
idea. There is one definite article, ***the***.

> Give me *the* book on the table.
> |
> a specific book   20
>
> I ate *the* apple from the garden.
> |
> a specific apple

The definite article remains *the* even when the noun that
follows becomes plural.

> Give me *the books* on the table.
> I ate *the apples* from the garden.

IN FRENCH

As in English, a definite article is used before a French   30
noun when referring to a specific person, place, animal,
thing, or idea.

> Donne-moi **le** livre sur la table.
> *Give me **the** book on the table.*
>
> J'ai mangé **la** pomme du jardin.
> *I ate **the** apple from the garden.*

Unlike English, however, there is more than one definite article. In French, the definite article works hand-in-hand with the noun to which it belongs in that it matches the noun's gender and number. This "matching" is called AGREEMENT. One says that "the article *agrees* with the noun." (See *What is Meant by Gender?*, p. 10 and *What is Meant by Number?*, p. 13).

A different article is used, therefore, depending on whether the noun is masculine or feminine (gender) and on whether the noun is singular or plural (number).

There are four forms of the definite article: three singular forms and one plural.

- **le** indicates that the noun is masculine singular

le livre	*the book*
le garçon	*the boy*

- **la** indicates that the noun is feminine singular

la table	*the table*
la pomme	*the apple*

- **l'** is used instead of **le** and **la** before a word beginning with a vowel.[1] It does not tell us if the noun is masculine or feminine.

l'étudiant	*the student*
|	
masculine	
l'université	*the university*
|	
feminine	

  Since the letter "h" is never pronounced, a word starting with "h" is usually considered as beginning with a vowel and uses **l'** as a definite article: **l'hiver** *(the winter)*; **l'hôtel** *(the hotel).* Your textbook will go into the few exceptions to this rule.

- **les** is used to indicate that the noun is plural. Since there is only one form, it does not tell us if the noun is masculine or feminine.

les livres	*the books*
les tables	*the tables*

---

[1]Vowels are the sounds associated with the letters *a, e, i (y), o* and *u;* consonants are the sounds associated with the other letters of the alphabet.

Because various forms of the articles are both pronounced and spelled differently, they indicate the gender
and number of the noun to the ear as well as to the eye
(see p. 14 regarding the "hearing" of the plural in French).

CAREFUL — French nouns often require the use of a definite
when none is expressed in English. Here are some examples.

- when the noun is used to speak in general terms.

  I like **chocolate***.*
  J'aime **le chocolat***.*

  Elephants *are strong.*
  Les éléphants *sont forts.*

- when the noun refers to a concept

  Time *is money.*
  Le temps, *c'est de l'argent.*

  Goodness *is worth more than* **beauty***.*
  La bonté *vaut mieux que* **la beauté***.*

- the names of countries and geographical areas

la France	France
le Portugal	Portugal
l'Allemagne	Germany
le Texas	Texas

Consult your textbook for exceptions and for more details
on the use of definite articles in French.

INDEFINITE ARTICLES
IN ENGLISH

An **INDEFINITE ARTICLE** is used before a noun when we are
not speaking about a specific person, animal, place,
thing, event, or idea. There are two indefinite articles, *a*
and *an.*

- *a* is used before a word beginning with a consonant

  I saw *a* boy in the street.

  not a specific boy

- *an* is used before a word beginning with a vowel

  I ate *an* apple.

  not a specific apple

The indefinite article is used only with a singular noun.
To indicate a non-specific plural noun, the word *some* or
any can be used, but it is usually left out.

I ate apples.
I ate *(some)* apples.

Do you have brothers and sisters?
Do you have *(any)* brothers and sisters?

IN FRENCH

As in English, an indefinite article is used before a French noun when referring to a non-specified person, place, animal, thing, or idea. Just as with French definite articles, indefinite articles must agree with the noun's gender and number. There are three forms of the indefinite article: two singular forms and one plural.

- **un** indicates that the noun is masculine singular

un livre	*a book*
un garçon	*a boy*

- **une** indicates that the noun is feminine singular

une table	*a table*
une pomme	*an apple*

- **des** is used to indicate that the noun is plural. Since there is only one form, it does not tell us if the noun is masculine or feminine. Unlike English where the plural definite article *some* can be omitted, the French equivalent **des** must be expressed.

des livres	*some books*
des tables	*some tables*

  J'ai mangé **des** pommes.
  *I ate (**some**) apples.*

Consult your textbook for exceptions and for more details on the use of indefinite articles in French.

CAREFUL — French nouns often require the use of a definite or indefinite article when none is expressed in English. Work on the assumption that all French nouns are preceded by an article of one sort or another. It is an exception when they are not.

PARTITIVE ARTICLES
IN FRENCH

In French there is also another set of articles called **PARTITIVE ARTICLES** so called because they refer to *"part* of the whole."* Partitive articles can be translated by the words *some* or *any*, but they are often left out in English.

Partitive articles are used before certain nouns called NON-COUNT NOUNS. As the name implies, a non-count noun designates an object that cannot be counted. For example, the noun *water* is a non-count noun because it is a noun that cannot be preceded by numbers such as 1, 2, 3, etc. (You cannot count *one water, two waters...*). Since a non-count noun cannot be counted, it is always singular.

Partitive articles are not used before COUNT NOUNS, nouns designating objects that can be counted. For example, the noun *pen* can be preceded by numbers such as 1, 2, 3, etc. (*one pen, two pens...*). Since a count noun can be counted, it can be singular or plural.

Like all articles in French, partitive articles agree with the noun's gender and number. Since non-count nouns don't have a plural form and are always singular, partitive articles only have singular forms.

There are three forms of the partitive article: masculine singular, feminine singular, and preceding a vowel. Unlike English where *some* or *any* can be omitted, the French partitive articles must be expressed.

- **du** indicates that the noun is masculine singular

    J'achète **du** beurre.
    *I am buying (**some**) butter.*

    Avez-vous **du** beurre?
    *Do you have (**any**) butter?*

- **de la** indicates that the noun is feminine singular

    J'achète **de la** viande.
    *I am buying (**some**) meat.*

    Avez-vous **de la** viande?
    *Do you have (**any**) meat?*

- **de l'** replaces **du** and **de la** before a noun beginning with a vowel. It does not tell us if the noun is masculine or feminine.

    Je bois **de l'**eau.
                    |
                feminine
    *I am drinking (**some**) water.*

    Devez-vous **de l'**argent?
                        |
                    masculine
    *Do you owe (**any**) money?*

The above is a brief summary of partitive articles. Refer to your textbook for rules regarding their usage.

Flashcards (see *Tips for Learning Vocabulary*, p. 1)

1. Make a flashcard for each new noun, listing the singular, and the plural if it is irregular, on the French side.
2. Use blue cards or blue pen for masculine nouns and red cards or red pen for feminine nouns. Associating the noun with blue or red will help you remember its gender.
3. Precede the noun with the appropriate definite article: **le, la** or **l'** (masc.) or **l'** (fem.).
4. Whether you're looking at the English or French side, as you say the French noun and article add an adjective such as "intéressant" (*interesting*) whose pronunciation changes according to whether it accompanies a masculine or feminine noun (in the masculine form the final "t" is not pronounced, in the feminine form it is.) The change in pronunciation of the adjective will reinforce the noun's gender in your memory.

le livre (intéressant)	*the book*
la maison (intéressante)	*the house*
l'année (fem.) (intéressante)	*the year*

5. Don't forget that it is only by repeated use that you will remember the words and their gender.

WHAT IS THE POSSESSIVE?

The term **POSSESSIVE** means that one noun owns or *possesses* another noun.

> Mary's French book is on the table.
> | |
> possessor   possessed

> The tree's branches are broken.
> | |
> possessor   possessed

IN ENGLISH

There are two constructions to show possession.

1. An apostrophe can be used. In this construction, the possessor comes before the possessed.

   - singular possessor adds an apostrophe + "s"

     Mary's dress
     a tree's branches
     |
     singular possessor

   - plural possessor ending with "s" adds an apostrophe after the "s"

     the students' teacher
     the girls' club
     |
     plural possessor

   - a plural possessor not ending with "s" adds an apostrophe + "s"

     the children's playground
     the men's department
     |
     plural possessor

2. The word *of* can be used. In this structure, the possessed comes before the possessor.

   - a singular or plural possessor is preceded by *of the* or *of a*

     the book *of the* professor
     the branches *of a* tree
                      |
            singular possessor

     the teacher *of the* students
                      |
            plural possessor

IN FRENCH

There is only one way to express possession and that is by using the "of" construction (2 above). The apostrophe structure (1 above) does not exist.

The French structure parallels the English structure: the noun possessed + **de** *(of)* + definite or indefinite article + the common noun possessor (if the possessor is a proper noun there is no preceding article).

Mary's dress	la robe **de** Marie
possessor possessed	possessed possessor
proper	*the dress **of** Mary*
noun	
the professor's book	le livre **du** professeur
possessor possessed	**de + le**
common	*the book **of** the professor*
noun	
the woman's purse	le sac **de la** dame
	*the purse **of the** lady*
a tree's branches	les branches **d'un** arbre
	*the branches **of a** tree*
the students' teacher	le professeur **des** étudiants
	de + les
	*the professor **of the** students*

CAREFUL — Do not confuse **du, de la, de l'**, and **des** used to show possession with words of the same spelling that are partitive and indefinite articles meaning *some* or *any* (pp. 18-9). When they come between two nouns they usually indicate possession: ***the book** of the **teacher** →* **le livre du professeur.** Otherwise they are articles.

7

WHAT IS A VERB?

A **VERB** is a word that indicates the action of the sentence. The word "action" is used in its broadest sense, not necessarily physical action.

Let us look at different types of words that are verbs:

- a physical activity   to run, to hit, to talk, to walk
- a mental activity   to hope, to believe, to imagine, to dream, to think
- a condition   to be, to feel, to have, to seem

Many verbs, however, do not fall neatly into one of the above three categories. They are verbs nevertheless because they represent the "action" of the sentence.

The book *costs* only $5.00.
     to cost

The students *seem* tired.
     to seem

The verb is the most important word in a sentence. You cannot write a **COMPLETE SENTENCE**, that is, express a complete thought, without a verb.

It is important to identify verbs because the function of words in a sentence often depends on their relationship to the verb. For instance, the subject of a sentence is the word doing the action of the verb and the object is the word receiving the action of the verb (see *What is a Subject?*, p. 28, and *What are Objects?*, p. 109).

IN ENGLISH

To help you learn to recognize verbs, look at the paragraph below where verbs are in *italics*.

The three students *entered* the restaurant, *selected* a table, *hung* up their coats and *sat* down. They *looked* at the menu and *asked* the waitress what she *recommended*. She *suggested* the daily special, beef stew. It *was* not expensive. They *chose* a bottle of red wine and *ordered* a salad. The service *was* slow, but the food *tasted* very good. Good cooking, they *decided*, *takes* time. They *ate* pastry for dessert and *ended* the meal with coffee. They *felt* happy!

IN FRENCH
Verbs are identified the same way as they are in English.

TERMS USED TO TALK ABOUT VERBS

- **INFINITIVE OR DICTIONARY FORM** — The verb form that is the name of the verb is called an infinitive: *to eat, to sleep, to drink* (see *What is the Infinitive?*, p. 25). In the dictionary a verb is listed without the "to": *eat, sleep, drink.*

- **CONJUGATION** — A verb is conjugated or changes form to agree with its subject: *I do, he does* (see *What is a Verb Conjugation?*, p. 37).

- **TENSE** — A verb indicates tense; that is, the time (present, past, or future) of the action: *I am, I was, I will be* (see *What is Meant by Tense?*, p. 53).

- **MOOD** — A verb shows mood; that is, the speaker's attitude toward what he or she is saying (see *What is Meant by Mood?*, p. 75).

- **VOICE** — A verb shows voice; that is, the relation between the subject and the action of the verb (see *What is Meant by Active and Passive Voice?*, p. 165).

- **PARTICIPLE** — A verb may be used to form a participle: *writing, written; singing, sung* (see *What is a Participle?*, p. 58).

- **TRANSITIVE OR INTRANSITIVE** — A verb can be classified as transitive or intransitive depending on whether or not the verb can take a direct object (see *What are Objects?*, p. 109).

STUDY TIPS — VERBS (SEE P. 27)

8

WHAT IS THE INFINITIVE?

The **INFINITIVE** form is the name of the verb.   1

> The French equivalent of the verb *to learn* is **étudier**.
>   infinitive

IN ENGLISH

The infinitive is composed of two words: *to* + the dictionary form of the verb *(to speak, to dance)*. By **DICTIONARY FORM** we mean the form of the verb that is listed as the entry in the dictionary *(speak, dance)*.

Although the infinitive is the most basic form of the verb, it can never be used in a sentence without another   10
verb that is conjugated (see *What is a Verb Conjugation?*, p. 37).

> ***To learn*** *is* exciting.
> infinitive conjugated verb

> It *is* important ***to be*** on time.
> conjugated verb   infinitive

> Paul and Mary *want* ***to dance*** together.   20
>   conjugated verb   infinitive

The dictionary form of the verb, rather than the infinitive, is used after a verb such as *must, let* and *can.*

> Paul *must **be*** home by noon.
>   dictionary form

> Mr. Smith *lets* his children ***watch*** television.
>   dictionary form

IN FRENCH   30

The infinitive form is usually shown by the last two or three letters of the verb called **THE ENDING**.

dan**ser**	*to dance*
fin**ir**	*to finish*
ven**dre**	*to sell*

The infinitive form is important not only because it is the form under which a verb is listed in the dictionary, but because the ending, called LA TERMINAISON, indicates the pattern the verb will follow to create its various forms.

1ST CONJUGATION — verbs ending in -**er** follow one pattern

2ND CONJUGATION — verbs ending in -**ir** follow another pattern

3RD CONJUGATION — verbs ending in -**re** follow another pattern

CONSULTING THE DICTIONARY

In English it is possible to change the meaning of a verb by placing short words (prepositions or adverbs) after it.

For example, the verb *look* in Column A below changes meaning depending on the word that follows it *(at, for, after, into)*. In French, it is impossible to change the meaning of a verb by adding a preposition or an adverb as in Column A. An entirely different French verb corresponds to each meaning.

COLUMN A		MEANING	FRENCH
to look	→	to look at	**regarder**
		I *looked at* the photo.	
to look *for*	→	to search for	**chercher**
		I *am looking for* a book.	
to look *after*	→	to take care of	**surveiller**
		I *am looking after* the children.	
to look *into*	→	to examine	**étudier**
		We*'ll look into* the problem.	

When consulting an English-French dictionary, all the examples under Column A can be found under the dictionary entry *look* (**regarder**); however, you will have to search under that entry for the specific expression *look for* (**chercher**), or *look after* (**surveiller**), to find the correct French equivalent.

Don't select the first entry under *look* and then add on the French equivalent for *after, for, into,* etc.; the result will be meaningless in French.

Flashcards (see *Tips for Learning Vocabulary*, p. 1)

1. Create flashcards indicating the infinitive form of the French verb on one side and its English equivalent on the other. You might want to select a particular color for verb cards so that later when you add information on the cards you can easily sort them out from the other cards (see Study Tips — *Verb conjugations*, p. 42; *Tenses*, p. 54; *The passé composé*, p. 65; *The future tense*, p. 72).

    finir   to finish

2. If the verb is a reflexive verb, indicate "se" before the infinitive (see *What are Reflexive Pronouns and Verbs?*, p. 129). If the verb can be used as a reflexive verb and as a non-reflexive verb, write both.

    se coucher   to go to bed
    Je me couche tôt.   I go to bed early.
    coucher   to put to bed
    Je couche les enfants.   I'm putting the children to bed.

3. If the verb is followed by the preposition "à" or can be part of a special construction, indicate it on the card with an example.

    répondre (à + person/thing)   to answer
    Je réponds à Marc.   I'm answering Marc.
    Je réponds au téléphone.   I'm answering the phone.

    dire (à + person + de + infinitive)   to tell someone to do something
    Marc dit à Pierre de partir.   Marc tells Peter to leave.

Practice

Follow the *Tips for Learning Vocabulary*, p. 1 to learn the French equivalent of English verbs. The real practice will come, however, when you learn to conjugate the verb and use the conjugated forms in sentences.

WHAT IS A SUBJECT?

The **SUBJECT** is the person or thing that performs the action of the verb. To find the subject, always look for the verb first, then ask *who?* or *what?* before the verb (see *What is a Verb?*, p. 23). The answer will be the subject.[1]

> *Paul* speaks French.
>> Verb: speaks
>> Who speaks French? Answer: Paul.
>> The subject refers to one person; it is singular (p. 13).

> Paul's *books* cost a lot of money.
>> Verb: cost
>> What costs a lot of money? Answer: books.
>> The subject refers to more than one thing; it is plural (p. 13).

If a verb has more than one subject, the subject is considered plural.

> *The book* and *the pencil* are on the table.
>> Verb: are
>> What is on the table? Answer: the book and the pencil.
>> The subject refers to more than one thing; it is plural.

If a sentence has more than one verb, you have to find the subject of each verb.

> *The boys* are cooking while *Mary* sets the table.
>> *Boys* is the plural subject of *are*.
>> *Mary* is the singular subject of *sets*.

IN ENGLISH

Always ask *who?* or *what?* before the verb to find the subject. Never assume that the first word in the sentence is the subject. Subjects can be located in several different places, as you can see in the following examples (the ***subject*** is in boldface and the *verb* italicized):

> Did ***the game*** *start* on time?
> After playing for two hours, ***Paul*** *became* exhausted.
> Mary's ***brothers*** from Chicago *arrived* yesterday.

---

[1]The subject performs the action in an active sentence, but is acted upon in a passive sentence (see *What is Meant by Active and Passive Voice?*, p. 165).

IN FRENCH

The subject is identified in the same way as it is in English. Also, as in English, it can be located in different places in the sentence.

CAREFUL — In both English and French it is important to find the subject of each verb to make sure that the verb form agrees with the subject (see *What is a Verb Conjugation?*, p. 37).

40

CHAPTER

10

WHAT IS A PRONOUN?

A **PRONOUN** is a word used to replace one or more nouns. Therefore it may stand for a person, animal, place, thing, event, or idea. For instance, rather than repeating the proper noun "Paul" in the following two sentences, it can be replaced by a pronoun in the second sentence.

> *Paul* likes to swim. *Paul* practices every day.
> *Paul* likes to swim. *He* practices every day.

The word that the pronoun replaces or refers to is called the **ANTECEDENT** of the pronoun. In the example above, the pronoun *he* refers to the proper noun *Paul. Paul* is the antecedent of the pronoun *he.*

There are different types of pronouns, each serving a different function and following different rules. Listed below are the more important types and the chapters in which they are discussed.

PERSONAL PRONOUNS — These pronouns replace nouns referring to persons or things which have been previously mentioned. A different set of pronouns is often used depending on the pronoun's function in the sentence.

■ as subject (see p. 32)

> *I* go; *they* read; *he* runs; *she* sings.

■ as direct object (see p. 116)

> Paul loves *it*. Jane met *him*.

■ as indirect object (see p. 118)

> Jane gave *us* the book. Speak to *them*.

■ as object of a preposition (see p. 125)

> Paul is going out with *her*.

■ as a disjunctive (see p. 123)

> Who is there? *Me*.

REFLEXIVE PRONOUNS — These pronouns refer back to the subject of the sentence (see p. 129).

> I cut *myself*. We washed *ourselves*. Mary dressed *herself*.

INTERROGATIVE PRONOUNS — These pronouns are used to ask questions (see p. 139).

> *Who* is that? *What* do you want?

DEMONSTRATIVE PRONOUNS — These pronouns are used to point out persons or things (see p. 160).

> *This (one)* is expensive. *That (one)* is cheap.

POSSESSIVE PRONOUNS — These pronouns are used to show possession (see p. 133).

> Whose book is that? *Mine. Yours* is on the table.

RELATIVE PRONOUNS — These pronouns are used to introduce relative clauses (see p. 147).

> The man *who* came is very nice.
> Where is the book *that* you read last summer?

INDEFINITE PRONOUNS — These pronouns are used to refer to unidentified persons or things.

> *One* doesn't do that.
> *Something* is wrong.

French indefinite pronouns correspond in usage to their English equivalents. They can be studied in your textbook.

IN ENGLISH

Each type of pronoun follows a different set of rules.

IN FRENCH

As in English, each type of pronoun follows a different set of rules. Moreover, French pronouns usually agree in gender and number with their antecedent.

CHAPTER

11

WHAT IS A SUBJECT PRONOUN?

A **SUBJECT PRONOUN** is a word which replaces a noun and that functions as a subject of a verb (see *What is a Subject?*, p. 28).

> *He* worked while *she* read.
>
> Who worked? Answer: He.
> *He* is the subject of the verb worked.
> Who read? Answer: She.
> *She* is the subject of the verb read.

Pronouns which refer to human beings or things are divided into three groups: 1st, 2nd, and 3rd person. The word **PERSON** in this instance does not necessarily mean a human being; it is a grammatical term which can refer to any noun.

IN ENGLISH

Here is a list of English subject pronouns grouped according to the person to which they belong.

1ST PERSON

I → person speaking → **SINGULAR**
we → person speaking plus others → **PLURAL**

Mary and I are free this evening. *We* are going out.

2ND PERSON

you → person or persons spoken to → **SINGULAR** or **PLURAL**

Paul, do *you* sing folk songs?
Peter, Paul and Mary, do *you* sing folk songs?

3RD PERSON

he, she, it → person or object spoken about → **SINGULAR**
they → persons or objects spoken about → **PLURAL**

Mary and Paul are free this evening. *They* are going out.

IN FRENCH

French subject pronouns are also grouped by person. They are presented in the following order:

SINGULAR

1ST PERSON	I	**je**
2ND PERSON	you	**tu**
3RD PERSON	he	**il**
	she	**elle**
	it	**il** or **elle**
	we	**on** (see **we** pp. 34-5)

1ˢᵀ PERSON	we	**nous**
2ⁿᴰ PERSON	you	**vous**
3ᴿᴰ PERSON	they	**ils** or **elles**

As you can see above, there are English subject pronouns which have more than one equivalent in French: *you* (**tu** or **vous**), *it* (**il** or **elle**), *we* (**nous** or **on**) and *they* (**ils** or **elles**). Let us look at each of these pronouns.

"YOU" (2ⁿᵈ person singular and plural)

tu (2ⁿᵈ person singular) or
vous (2ⁿᵈ person plural)

IN ENGLISH

The pronoun "you" is used to address one or more than one person.

> Mary, are *you* coming with me?
> Mary and Paul, are *you* coming with me?

The same pronoun "you" is used to address the President of the United States or your dog.

> Do *you* have any questions, Mr. President?
> *You* are a good dog, Heidi.

IN FRENCH

When you are addressing one person there are two forms, depending on the person you're speaking to and on whether or not you are on familiar terms with him or her.

- when speaking to a child, an animal, a family member, a friend, or anyone with whom you are on familiar terms, use the FAMILIAR FORM → TU (2ⁿᵈ person singular).

> *Mom, are **you** coming with us?*
> |
>   **tu**

- when speaking to a person with whom you are not on familiar terms, use the FORMAL FORM or the POLITE FORM → VOUS (2ⁿᵈ person plural). Notice that even though the form is plural, it is used to address one person.

> *Mrs. Smith, are **you** coming with us?*
> |
>   **vous**

When you are speaking to an adult and unsure which form to use, use **vous**.

80

When you are addressing more than one person whether you are on familiar terms with them or not, there is only one form → **vous** (2ⁿᵈ person plural).

> *Mom and Dad, are **you** coming with us?*
> |
>   vous

> *Mr. and Mrs. Smith, are **you** coming with us?*
> |
>   vous

"IT" (3ʳᵈ person singular)

90

il (3ʳᵈ person singular masculine) or
elle (3ʳᵈ person singular feminine)

IN ENGLISH

The pronoun "it" is used whenever you are speaking about one thing or idea.

> Where is the book? *It* is on the table.
> Here is the chair. *It* is comfortable.

IN FRENCH

100

The subject pronoun used depends on the gender of its ANTECEDENT, that is, the noun it replaces.

- masculine antecedent → **il**

> Où est le livre? **Il** est sur la table.
> | |
>   masc. sing. masc. sing.
>   antecedent pronoun
> *Where is the book? **It** is on the table.*

- feminine antecedent → **elle**

> Voici la chaise. **Elle** est confortable.
> | |
>   fem. sing.   fem. sing.

110

>   antecedent   pronoun
> *Here is the chair. **It** is comfortable.*

"WE"(1ˢᵗ person plural)

nous (1ˢᵗ person plural) or
on (3ʳᵈ person singular)

IN ENGLISH

The subject pronoun "we" is used when you are speaking about yourself and one or more other persons.

> Paul and I are students; *we* study a lot.

120

> I studied with friends; *we* passed the exam.

IN FRENCH

The subject pronoun used is either the 1ˢᵗ person plural pronoun **nous** or, in spoken French, the 3ʳᵈ person singular pronoun **on**. Depending on which of these two pronouns is used, the verb form will be in either in the 1ˢᵗ person plural for **nous** or in the 3ʳᵈ person singular for **on** (see p. 38 in *What is a Verb Conjugation?*).

> *We study a lot.*
> **Nous étudions** beaucoup.   130
> |
>   1ˢᵗ pers. pl.
> **On étudie** beaucoup.
> |
>   3ʳᵈ pers. sing.

Consult your textbook for other usages of the pronoun **on**, remembering that regardless of its English equivalent the French verb is always in the 3ʳᵈ person singular.

"THEY" (3ʳᵈ person plural)

> **ils** (3ʳᵈ person plural masculine) or
> **elles** (3ʳᵈ person plural feminine)   140

IN ENGLISH

The subject pronoun "they" is used when you are speaking about more than one person or object.

> Paul and Henry are students; *they* study a lot.
> Where are the books? *They* are on the table.

IN FRENCH

The subject pronoun used depends on the gender of its ANTECEDENT, that is, the noun it replaces.

                                                          150
- masculine antecedent → **ils**

> Où sont les livres? **Ils** sont sur la table.
> | |
>   masc. pl.   masc. pl.
>   antecedent   pronoun
> *Where are the books? **They** are on the table.*

> Paul et Henri sont étudiants; **ils** étudient beaucoup.
> | | |
> masc. sing. + masc. sing.   masc. pl.
>   └─ antecedents ─┘   pronoun
> *Paul and Henry are students. **They** study a lot.*

                                                          160
> Où sont le livre et le cahier? **Ils** sont sur la table.
> | | |
>   masc. sing. + masc. sing.   masc. pl.
>   └─ antecedents ─┘   pronoun
> *Where are the book and the notebook? **They** are on the table.*

■ feminine antecedent → **elles**

Voici les chaises; **elles** sont confortables.

fem. pl.   fem. pl.
antecedent pronoun

*Here are the chairs; **they** are comfortable.*

Anne et Marie sont étudiantes; **elles** étudient beaucoup.

fem. sing. + fem. sing.   fem. pl.
└─ antecedents ─┘   pronoun

*Anne and Mary are students. **They** study a lot.*

Où sont la clé et la montre? **Elles** sont sur la table.

fem. sing. + fem. sing.   fem. pl.
└─ antecedents ─┘   pronoun

*Where are the key and the watch? **They** are on the table.*

■ antecedents of different genders → **ils**

Voici la clé et le cahier. **Ils** sont sur la table.

fem. sing. + masc. sing.   masc. pl.
└─ antecedents ─┘   pronoun

*Here are the key and the notebook. **They** are on the table.*

STUDY TIPS — SUBJECT PRONOUNS

Flashcards
Create a flashcard for each subject pronoun (1st, 2nd, and 3rd person singular and plural). You'll add the other forms of the pronoun when you learn them (see *Study Tips — Object Pronouns*, p. 122).

je   *I*
il   *he, it*

Practice
You'll practice subject pronouns when you practice conjugating verbs (see *Study Tips — Verb Conjugations*, p. 42).

WHAT IS A VERB CONJUGATION?

A **VERB CONJUGATION** is a list of the six possible forms of the verb for a particular tense. For each tense, there is one verb form for each of the pronouns used as the subject of the verb (see *What is Meant by Tense?*, p. 53).

> I am
> you are
> he, she, it is
> we are
> you are
> they are

Different tenses have different verb forms, but the principle of conjugation remains the same. In this chapter all our examples are in the present tense (see *What is the Present Tense?*, p. 56).

IN ENGLISH

The verb *to be* is the English verb that changes the most; it has three forms: *am, are,* and *is.* (The initial vowel is often replaced by an apostrophe: *I'm, you're, he's.*) Other English verbs only have two forms: *to sing,* for instance.

SINGULAR

1ST PERSON	I *sing*
2ND PERSON	you *sing*
3RD PERSON	he *sings* she *sings* it *sings*

PLURAL

1ST PERSON	we *sing*
2ND PERSON	you *sing*
3RD PERSON	they *sing*

Because English verbs change so little, it isn't necessary to learn "to conjugate a verb;" that is, to list all its possible forms. For most verbs, it is much simpler to say that the verb adds an "-s" in the 3rd person singular (see p. 32).

IN FRENCH

Unlike English, French verb forms change from one person to another so that when you learn a new verb you must also learn how to conjugate it. First, you must establish whether the verb is regular or irregular.

- Verbs whose forms follow a pattern are called REGULAR VERBS. Only one example must be memorized and the pattern can then be applied to other verbs in the same group.
- Verbs whose forms do not follow a pattern are called IRREGULAR VERBS and must be memorized individually. Unfortunately, this is the case of the most commonly used French verbs.

The forms of a verb, whether regular or irregular, are memorized with subject pronouns and the verb form that agrees with that subject pronoun. This list of subject pronouns and corresponding verb form is referred to as the conjugation of the verb.

CHOOSING THE PROPER "PERSON" (see p. 32)

Below is the conjugation of the regular verb **chanter** *(to sing)*. Notice that each of the six persons has its own ending and that different pronouns belonging to the same person have the same verb form. For instance, the 3rd person singular has three pronouns, **il**, **elle**, **on**, but they have the same verb form: **chante**.

SINGULAR

1ST PERSON	je chante	*I sing*
2ND PERSON	tu chantes	*you sing*
3RD PERSON	il chante	*he sings, it sings*
	elle chante	*she sings, it sings*
	on chante	*we sing* (see p. 35)

PLURAL

1ST PERSON	nous chantons	*we sing*
2ND PERSON	vous chantez	*you sing*
3RD PERSON	ils chantent	*they sing*
	elles chantent	*they sing*

To choose the proper verb form, you must identify the person (1st, 2nd or 3rd) and the number (singular or plural) of the subject.

1ST PERSON SINGULAR — The subject is always **je** *(I)*.

Le matin **je chante** bien.
*In the morning **I sing** well.*

2ND PERSON SINGULAR — The subject is always **tu** *(you)*.

Jean, **tu chantes** bien.
*John, **you sing** well.*

3RD PERSON SINGULAR — The subject can be expressed in one of four ways:

80

1. a proper noun

> **Marie chante** bien.
> |
> feminine → **elle** *(she)*
> ***Mary sings*** *well.*

> **Paul chante** bien.
> |
> masculine → **il** *(he)*
> ***Paul sings*** *well.*

90

> > In both sentences the proper noun could be replaced by the pronoun *she* (**elle** → fem.) or *he* (**il** → masc.), so you must use the 3rd person singular form of the verb.

2. a singular common noun

> **La fille chante** bien.
> |
> feminine → **elle** *(she)*
> ***The girl sings*** *well.*

> **L'oiseau chante** bien.
> |
> masculine → **il** *(it)*
> ***The bird sings*** *well.*

100

> > In both sentences the common noun could be replaced by the pronoun *she* (**elle** → fem.) or *it* (**il** → masc.), so you must use the 3rd person singular form of the verb.

3. the 3rd person singular masculine pronoun **il** *(he, it)* or the 3rd person singular feminine pronoun **elle** *(she, it)*

> Paul aime chanter. **Il chante** bien.
> | |
> masc.   masc.
> *Paul likes to sing.* ***He sings*** *well.*

110

> Regardez ce livre. **Il est** intéressant.
> | |
>   masc. masc.
> *Look at this book.* ***It is*** *interesting.*

> Marie aime chanter. **Elle chante** bien.
> | |
> fem.   fem.
> *Mary likes to sing.* ***She sings*** *well.*

> Voici la chaise. **Elle est** confortable.
> | |
>   fem. fem.
> *Here is the chair.* ***It is*** *comfortable.*

120

4. the 3rd person singular pronoun **on** *(we, see p. 35)*

> **On chante** bien.
> |
> 3rd pers. sing.
> *We sing well.*
> |
> 1st pers. pl.

1ST PERSON PLURAL — The subject can be expressed in one of two ways:

1. a multiple subject in which the speaker is included

> **Marie, Paul et moi chantons** bien.
> └————————┘
> nous
> *Mary, Paul and I sing well.*
>
> The subject, *Mary, Paul* and *I,* could be replaced by the pronoun *we,* so that you must use the 1st person plural form of the verb.

2. the first person plural pronoun **nous** *(we)*

> **Nous chantons** bien.
> *We sing well.*

2ND PERSON PLURAL — The subject is always **vous** *(you).*

> Madame Dupont, **vous chantez** bien.
> *Mrs. Dupont, you sing well.*

3RD PERSON PLURAL — The subject can be expressed in one of three ways:

1. a plural noun

> **Les filles chantent** bien.
> |
> feminine pl. → **elles** *(they)*
> *The girls sing well.*

2. two or more proper or common nouns

> **Marie et Hélène chantent** bien.
> └————┘
> fem. + fem. → **elles** *(they)*
> *Mary and Helen sing well.*
>
> **La fille et le garçon chantent** bien.
> └————┬————┘
> fem. + masc. → **ils** *(they)*
> *The girl and the boy sing well.*

3. the 3rd person plural masculine pronoun **ils** *(they)* or the 3rd person plural feminine pronoun **elles** *(they)*

> **Paul et Henri aiment** chanter. **Ils chantent** bien.
> └————┘ |
> masc. + masc. → **ils** *(they)*   masc. pl.
> *Paul and Henry like to sing. They sing well.*

130

140

150

160

Regardez ces livres. **Ils sont** intéressants.
      | |
      masc. pl. masc. pl.
*Look at these books. **They are** interesting.*

Marie et Hélène aiment chanter. **Elles chantent** bien.
      |_____| |
      fem. + fem. → **elles** *(they)*   fem. pl.   170
***Mary and Helen like** to sing. **They sing** well.*

Voici les chaises. **Elles sont** confortables.
      | |
      fem. pl.   fem. pl.
*Here are the chairs. **They are** comfortable.*

How to conjugate a verb

A French verb, whether regular or irregular, is composed of two parts:

1. the **stem**, "**la racine**" in French, is found by dropping   180
   the last two letters from the infinitive (see *What is the Infinitive?*, p. 25).

Infinitive	Stem
chant**er**	chant-
fin**ir**	fin-
vend**re**	vend-

The stem of regular verbs usually remains the same throughout a conjugation. You will have to memorize the changes in the stem of irregular verbs.

190

2. the **ending**, "**la terminaison**" in French, changes for each person in the conjugation of regular and irregular verbs.

Regular verbs are divided into three **groups**, also called **conjugations**, identified by the last two letters of the infinitive ending of the verb.

-er	-ir	-re
1st group	2nd group	3rd group

Each of the three verb groups has its own set of endings   200
for each tense (see *What is Meant by Tense?*, p. 53). Memorizing the conjugation of one sample verb for each tense of each group enables you to conjugate in the various tenses the other regular verbs belonging to that group.

As an example of the steps to follow to conjugate a regular verb, let us look at verbs of the 1st group (-**er** verbs); that is, verbs like **parler** (*to speak*) and **aimer** (*to love*) that follow the pattern of **chanter** (*to sing*) conjugated on p. 38.

1. Identify the group of the verb by its infinitive ending.

parl**er**	→1ˢᵗ conjugation or group
aim**er**	

2. Find the verb stem by removing the infinitive ending.

parl-
aim-

3. Add the ending that agrees with the subject.

je parle	j'aime
tu parles	tu aimes
il parle	il aime
elle parle	elle aime
on parle	on aime
nous parlons	nous aimons
vous parlez	vous aimez
ils parlent	ils aiment
elles parlent	elles aiment

The endings of regular verbs belonging to the other groups are different, but the process of conjugation is the same. Just follow the three steps above.

As irregular verbs are introduced in your textbook, their entire conjugation will be given so that you can memorize them individually. Be sure to do so because many common verbs are irregular (**avoir**, *to have*; **être**, *to be*; **aller**, *to go;* and **faire**, *to make*, for example).

CAREFUL — French verb forms are often pronounced the same way, but written differently (for instance, *parle, parles, parlent*). The only way to write the proper ending of a verb is to identify its subject.

STUDY TIPS — VERB CONJUGATIONS

Pattern (see *Tips for Learning Word Forms*, p. 3)
1. Start by looking for a pattern within the conjugation of the verb itself. For example, let's find a pattern in the irregular verb **faire** *(to make, to do)*.

je fais	nous faisons
tu fais	vous faites
il/elle/on fait	ils/elles font

What pattern do you see?
- all the forms start with **fai-** except the **ils/elles** form
- **je** and **tu** have the same ending, - s
2. As you learn new verbs, look for similarities with other conjugations. For instance, make a list of the similarities between the conjugation of **faire, partir** *(to leave)*, **avoir** *(to have)* and **être** *(to be)*. When you've finished, compare your list to the one on the next page.

je pars	nous partons	j'ai	nous avons	je suis	nous sommes
tu pars	vous partez	tu as	vous avez	tu es	vous êtes
il/elle part	ils/elles partent	il/elle a	ils/elles ont	il/elle est	ils/elles sont

What similarities did you see? Compare your list to the one below.

- singular forms of **faire** have the same endings as the singular forms of **partir** and **être**: -s, -s, -t (you will find this pattern in many other verbs)
- all the **tu** forms end with -s (like most regular verbs)
- **nous** form of **faire, partir, avoir** ends with -**ons** (like most regular verbs)
- **vous** form of **partir** and **avoir** ends in -**ez** (like most regular verbs)
- **vous** form of **faire** and **être** ends in -**tes**
- **ils/elles** form of **faire** and **être** ends in -**ont**, which is the **ils/elles** form of **avoir**

4. As new verb conjugations are introduced, more and more similarities and patterns will become evident. Take the time to look for them; it will make learning conjugations much easier and faster.

Practice

1. As you learn the different forms of a verb, write them down (always using the subject pronoun) as many times as you need to so that you can do so without referring to your textbook.
2. Apply the pattern you've just learned to another verb of the same conjugation, if there is one.
3. Practice using the various forms out of order, so that if you are asked a question you can respond without going through the entire pattern.
4. Be sure to do the exercises that follow the introduction of a new conjugation. When you've finished, refer to your textbook or answer key to make corrections. Mark the mistakes and corrections with a colored pen so that they stand out when you review.
5. Write your own sentences using the different forms of the verb, or preferably with other verbs that are conjugated the same way.

Flashcards

To review verbs and their conjugation, take out the flashcards you created to learn the meaning of verbs (see p. 27) and add the following information on the French side:

1. Indicate if the verb is (reg.) or irregular (irreg.) so that you can review irregular verbs separately.

| parler | *to speak (reg.)* |
| être | *to be (irreg.)* |

2. If it is a regular verb with spelling irregularities, indicate the irregularity.

| manger | *to eat* |
| nous mangeons | *we eat* |

3. If the verb is irregular but shares a pattern with another verb, indicate the other verb.

| dormir | *to sleep (like* partir = *to leave)* |

4. For irregular verbs, write down the **je, nous** and **ils** forms, as the other forms can usually be deduced from them.

boire	*to drink*
je bois, nous buvons,	*I drink, we drink,*
ils boivent	*they drink*

See also *Study Tips — Tenses* (p. 54).

CHAPTER

13

WHAT ARE AUXILIARY VERBS?

An **AUXILIARY VERB** or **HELPING VERB** is a verb that helps another verb, called the **MAIN VERB,** form one of its tenses.

He *has been* gone two weeks.	*has*	AUXILIARY VERB
	been	AUXILIARY VERB
	gone	MAIN VERB

IN ENGLISH

There are three auxiliary verbs, *to have, to be*, and *to do*, as well as a series of auxiliary words such as *will, would, may, must, can, could*, that are used to change the tense and meaning of the main verb.

- Auxiliaries are used primarily to indicate the tense of the main verb (present, past, future — see *What is Meant by Tense?*, p. 53).

Mary *is* reading a book.   PRESENT
auxiliary *to be*

Mary *has* read a book.   PAST
auxiliary *to have*

Mary *will* read a book.   FUTURE
auxiliary *will*

- The auxiliary verb *to do* is used to help formulate questions and to make sentences negative (see *What are Affirmative and Negative Sentences?*, p. 47 and *What are Declarative and Interrogative Sentences?*, p. 50).

Does Mary *read* a book?   INTERROGATIVE SENTENCE
Mary *does not* read a book.   NEGATIVE SENTENCE

IN FRENCH

There are only two auxiliary verbs: **avoir** (*to have*) and **être** (*to be*). They are used to change the tense of the main verb.

The other English auxiliaries such as *do, does, did, will* or *would* do not exist as auxiliaries in French. Their meaning is conveyed either by a different structure or by a form of the main verb. You will find more on this subject under the chapters dealing with the different tenses.

The verbs **avoir** and **être** are irregular verbs whose conjugations must be memorized. They are important verbs
because they serve both as auxiliary verbs and main verbs.   40

J'**ai** ce livre.	**avoir** *(to have)*	MAIN VERB
I have that book.		
J'**ai acheté** ce livre.	**avoir**	AUXILIARY VERB
I bought that book.	acheter *(to buy)*	MAIN VERB
Je **suis** à la maison.	**être** *(to be)*	MAIN VERB
I am at home.		
Je **suis allé** à la maison.	**être**	AUXILIARY VERB
I went home.	aller *(to go)*	MAIN VERB

A verb tense composed of an auxiliary verb plus a main   50
verb is called a **COMPOUND TENSE**, as opposed to a **SIMPLE
TENSE** that is a tense composed of only the main verb.

Je **mange.**
simple tense
present of **manger**
I eat.

J'**ai mangé.**
auxiliary main
verb   verb
compound tense   60
past tense of **manger**
I have eaten.

AUXILIARY VERBS ARE USED TO INDICATE TENSE

Verbs take either **avoir** or **être** as auxiliary to form all of
their compound tenses (see p. 62 for guidelines on
selecting the proper auxiliary). The auxiliary, conjugated
in the different tenses, and the past participle of the main
verb (see *What is a Participle?*, p. 58) form the various tenses
of the main verb.   70

Let us look at examples of some compound tenses. The
first sentence of each pair is a verb that takes a form of
avoir as auxiliary (**manger,** *to eat)* and the second a verb
that takes a form of **être** as auxiliary (**aller,** *to go).*

PASSÉ COMPOSÉ (PRESENT PERFECT) — Present of **avoir** or **être**
+ past participle of main verb (see *What is the Past Tense?*,
p. 61). There are two possible English equivalents.

Le garçon **a mangé** la pomme.
*The boy **ate (has eaten)** the apple.*

80
La fille **est allée** au cinéma.
*The girl **went (has gone)** to the movies.*

PLUS-QUE-PARFAIT (PAST PERFECT) — Imperfect of **avoir** or **être** + past participle of main verb (see *What is the Past Perfect Tense?*, p. 67).

Le garçon **avait mangé** la pomme.
*The boy **had eaten** the apple.*

La fille **était allée** au cinéma.
*The girl **had gone** to the movies.*

90
FUTUR ANTÉRIEUR (FUTURE PERFECT) — Future of **avoir** or **être** + past participle of main verb (see *What is the Future Perfect Tense?*, p. 73).

Le garçon **aura mangé** la pomme.
*The boy **will have eaten** the apple.*

La fille **sera allée** au cinéma.
*The girl **will have gone** to the movies.*

CONDITIONNEL PASSÉ (PAST CONDITIONAL) — Conditional of **avoir** or **être** + past participle of main verb (see pp. 80-1 in
100
What is the Conditional?).

Le garçon **aurait mangé** la pomme.
*The boy **would have eaten** the apple.*

La fille **serait allée** au cinéma.
*The girl **would have gone** to the movies.*

You will learn other compound tenses as your study of French progresses.

WHAT ARE AFFIRMATIVE AND NEGATIVE SENTENCES?

A sentence can be classified according to whether or not the
verb is negated, that is, made negative with the word *not*.

An AFFIRMATIVE SENTENCE is a sentence whose verb is not
negated.

> France *is* a country in Europe.
> Paul *will work* at the university.
> They *liked* to travel.

A NEGATIVE SENTENCE is a sentence whose verb is negated with
the word ***not***.

> France *is not* a country in Asia.
> Paul *will not* work at the university.
> They *did not like* to travel.

IN ENGLISH

An affirmative sentence can be made negative in one or
two ways:

1. by adding ***not*** after auxiliary verbs or auxiliary words
   (see *What are Auxiliary Verbs?*, p. 44)

AFFIRMATIVE	NEGATIVE
Paul *is* a student.	Paul *is not* a student.
Mary *can* do it.	Mary *cannot* do it.
They *will* travel.	They *will not* travel.

   The word *not* is often attached to the auxiliary and the
   letter "o" is replaced by an apostrophe; this is called a CON-
   TRACTION: *is not* → *isn't; cannot* → *can't; will not* → *won't.*

2. by adding the auxiliary verb ***do, does,*** or ***did + not*** and
   giving the dictionary form of the main verb

AFFIRMATIVE	NEGATIVE
We *study* a lot.	We *do not study* a lot.
Mary *writes* well.	Mary *does not write* well.
The train *arrived.*	The train *did not arrive.*

   Frequently, *do, does,* or *did* is contracted with *not: do not*
   → *don't; does not* → *doesn't; did not* → *didn't.*

IN FRENCH

An affirmative sentence is made negative by putting **ne**
(**n'** before a vowel) right after the subject and the negative
pas *(not)* after the conjugated verb.

1

10

20

30

AFFIRMATIVE	NEGATIVE
Elles **mangent** beaucoup.	Elles **ne** mangent **pas** beaucoup.
They eat a lot.	conjugated verb
	They do not eat a lot.

Marie **écrit** bien.	Marie **n'**écrit **pas** bien.
Mary writes well.	conjugated verb
	Mary does not write well.

Le train **est** arrivé.	Le train **n'**est **pas** arrivé.
The train arrived.	conjugated verb
	The train did not arrive.

CAREFUL — Remember that there is no equivalent for the auxiliary words *do, does, did* in French; do not try to include them in negative sentences.

NEGATIVE WORDS

In both English and French there are other negative words besides *not*. These negatives can function as either object or subject of the sentence.

IN ENGLISH

The most common negative words are: *nothing, nobody, no one, never. Nothing* and *no one (nobody)* are often used as objects or subjects of a sentence.

- object of the sentence

    I have *nothing* to give you.
    Before the exam he sees *no one (nobody)*.

- subject of the sentence

    Nothing is free.
    No one is going on vacation.

IN FRENCH

The most common negative words are: **rien** *(nothing)*, **personne** *(nobody, no one)* and **jamais** *(never)*. They are always used with **ne**; however, the placement of **ne** changes depending on whether **rien** or **personne** is used as an object or a subject of a sentence.

- object of the sentence → subject + **ne** + conjugated verb + **rien** or **personne** (same as **ne...pas** above)

    Je **n'**ai **rien** à donner.
    *I have **nothing** to give.*

Avant l'examen il **ne** voit **personne**.
*Before the exam he sees **no one (nobody)**.*

Il **n'**arrive **jamais** à l'heure.
*He **never** arrives on time.*

80

- subject of the sentence → **rien ne** or **personne ne** + verb

   Rien n'est gratuit.
   ***Nothing** is free.*

   Personne ne part en vacances.
   ***No one** is going on holiday.*

The position of **ne** and the negative word in a sentence also changes depending on the tense of the verb. Consult your French textbook.

CHAPTER

15

WHAT ARE DECLARATIVE AND INTERROGATIVE SENTENCES?

A sentence can be classified as to whether it is making a statement or asking a question.

A **DECLARATIVE SENTENCE** is a sentence that makes a statement.

> Columbus discovered America in 1492.

An **INTERROGATIVE SENTENCE** is a sentence that asks a question.

> Did Columbus discover America in 1492?

In written language, an interrogative sentence always ends with a question mark.

IN ENGLISH

A declarative sentence can be changed to an interrogative sentence in one of two ways:

1. by adding the auxiliary verb *do, does*, or *did* before the subject and giving the dictionary form of the main verb.

DECLARATIVE SENTENCE	INTERROGATIVE SENTENCE
Philip *likes* the class.	*Does* Philip *like* the class?
Paul and Mary *sing* well.	*Do* Paul and Mary *sing* well?
Alice *went* to Paris.	*Did* Alice *go* to Paris?

2. by inverting the normal word order of subject + verb to verb + subject. This **INVERSION** can only be used with auxiliary verbs or auxiliary words (see *What are Auxiliary Verbs?*, p. 44).

DECLARATIVE SENTENCE	INTERROGATIVE SENTENCE
Paul is home.	*Is Paul* home?
You have received a letter.	*Have you received* a letter?
She will come tomorrow.	*Will she come* tomorrow?

IN FRENCH

A declarative sentence can be changed to an interrogative sentence in one of two ways:

1. by adding the expression **est-ce que** before the complete declarative sentence

> **Est-ce que** je peux manger maintenant?
> *I can eat now*
> complete declarative sentence
>
> *Can I eat now?*

Est-ce que Paul mange à la maison?
> *Paul eats at home*
> └─────────┬─────────┘
> complete declarative sentence

Does Paul eat at home?

2. by using the inversion form; that is, by putting any pro- 40
noun subject, except **je**, after the verb. (If **je** is the subject, the **est-ce que** form is used.)

- when the subject is a pronoun, simply invert the verb
and pronoun subject

  Vous mangez à la maison ce soir.
  Mangez-vous à la maison ce soir?
  You are eating at home this evening.
  Are you eating at home this evening?

- when the subject is a noun, follow these steps: 50
  1. State the noun subject.
  2. State the verb and, when writing, add a hyphen.
  3. State the subject pronoun that corresponds to the
     gender and number of the subject (see pp. 32-6).

Let's look at a few examples.

Paul est-il à la maison?
> (word-for-word: ***Paul is he** home*)

Is Paul home?

La montre et la clé sont-elles sur la table? 60
> (word-for-word: ***the watch and the key** are **they** on the table*)
> Since both subjects (**la montre** and **la clé**) are feminine,
> the pronoun will be feminine plural → **elles**.

Are the watch and the key on the table?

Paul et Marie étudient-ils ensemble?
> (word-for-word: ***Paul and Mary** do **they** study together*)
> Since one subject is masculine (**Paul**) and the other feminine
> (**Marie**), the pronoun will be masculine plural → **ils** (see p. 36).

Do Paul and Mary study together?

When a verb ending with a vowel in the 3rd person singular is inverted, -t- is added between the verb and sub- 70
ject pronoun to facilitate pronunciation.

Paul **aime-t-il** ses cours à l'université?
Does Paul like his classes at the university?

Marie **va-t-elle** manger au restaurant?
Is Mary going to eat at the restaurant?

Consult your textbook for more information.

CAREFUL — When *do, does,* or *did* are used as auxiliaries make sure that you do not translate them. Just like the expression **est-ce que**, they are used to turn the complete
80   sentence which follows into a question.

TAG QUESTIONS

In both English and French when you expect a yes-or-no answer, you can also transform a statement into a question by adding a short phrase at the end of the statement. This short phrase is called a TAG.

IN ENGLISH

There are many different tags, depending on factors such as the tense of the verb in the statement and whether the
90   statement is affirmative or negative. For instance, affirmative statements take negative tags and negative statements take affirmative tags.

> Paul and Mary *study* together, *don't they?*
> Paul and Mary *don't study* together, *do they?*

IN FRENCH

There is only one tag, **n'est-ce pas?** It can be added to any statement requiring a yes-or-no answer to turn it into a question.

100

> Paul et Marie étudient ensemble, **n'est-ce pas?**
> *Paul and Mary study together, **don't they?***
>
> Paul et Marie n'étudient pas ensemble, **n'est-ce pas?**
> *Paul and Mary don't study together, **do they?***

WHAT IS MEANT BY TENSE?

The TENSE of a verb indicates when the action of the verb takes place: at the present time, in the past, or in the future. The word *tense* comes from the same word as the French word "temps," which means *time*.

1

I am eating.	PRESENT
I ate.	PAST
I will eat.	FUTURE

As you can see in the above examples, just by putting the verb in a different tense and without giving any additional information (such as "I am eating *now*," "I ate *yesterday*," "I will eat *tomorrow*"), you can indicate when the action of the verb takes place.

10

Tenses may be classified according to the way they are formed. A SIMPLE TENSE consists of only one verb form (I *ate*), while a COMPOUND TENSE consists of one or more auxiliaries plus the main verb (I *am eating*).

In this section we will only consider tenses of the indicative mood (see *What is Meant by Mood?*, p. 75).

IN ENGLISH

20

Listed below are the main tenses of the indicative mood whose equivalents you will encounter in French:

PRESENT

I study	PRESENT
I do study	PRESENT EMPHATIC
I am studying	PRESENT PROGRESSIVE

PAST

I studied	SIMPLE PAST
I did study	PAST EMPHATIC
I have studied	PRESENT PERFECT
I had studied	PAST PERFECT
I was studying	PAST PROGRESSIVE

30

FUTURE

| I will study | FUTURE |
| I will have studied | FUTURE PERFECT |

As you can see, there are only two simple tenses (present and simple past); all of the other tenses are compound tenses.

IN FRENCH

Listed below are the main tenses of the indicative mood that you will encounter in French:

PRESENT

| j'étudie | *I study, I am studying*
I do study | PRÉSENT (PRESENT) |

PAST

j'ai étudié	*I studied, I have studied* *I did study*	PASSÉ COMPOSÉ (PRESENT PERFECT)
j'étudiais	*I was studying,* *I used to study*	IMPARFAIT (IMPERFECT)
j'avais étudié	*I had studied*	PLUS-QUE-PARFAIT (PAST PERFECT)

FUTURE

| j'étudierai | *I will study* | FUTUR (FUTURE) |
| j'aurai étudié | *I will have studied* | FUTUR ANTÉRIEUR (FUTURE PERFECT) |

As you can see, there are more simple tenses in French than in English: present, imperfect, future. French compound tenses are formed with the auxiliary verbs **avoir** *(to have)* or **être** *(to be)* + the past participle of the main verb. (The verb **étudier** above uses the auxiliary verb **avoir** to form its compound tenses.)

This handbook discusses the various tenses and their usage in separate chapters: *What is the Present Tense?*, p. 56; *What is the Past Tense?*, p. 61; *What is the Past Perfect Tense?*, p. 67; *What is the Future Tense?*, p. 70; and *What is the Future Perfect Tense?*, p. 73. Verb tenses can be grouped according to the mood to which they belong (see *What is Meant by Mood?*, p. 75).

CAREFUL — Do not assume that tenses with the same name in English and in French are used in the same way.

STUDY TIPS — TENSES

Pattern (see *Tips for Learning Word Forms,* p. 3)
1. Start by comparing the forms of the new tense to the other forms of that verb you already know, particularly the forms that are close in spelling and/or pronunciation.
   ■ Identify the similarities with the other tenses. This will help you remember the new tense.
   ■ Identify the differences with the other tenses. This will help you avoid mixing them up.
2. Remember that a verb that is irregular in one tense is not necessarily irregular in another.

Practice

1. To learn the forms of a simple tense, follow the instructions *Study Tips — Verb conjugation*, p. 42.
2. To learn the forms of a compound tense, follow the instructions *Study Tips — The* **passé composé**, p. 65.
3. Apply the pattern you've just learned by writing and saying aloud another verb that follows the same pattern.
4. Rewrite the practice sentences of a tense you've learned earlier using the new tense.

Flashcards

As you learn new tenses, sort out the verbs from your other cards and note any irregularities on the French side.

vouloir	*to want* (infinitive, see *Study Tips*, p. 27)
je veux	*I want*
nous voulons	*we want*
ils veulent	*they want* (present, see *Study Tips*, p. 42)
j'ai voulu	*I wanted, I tried to* + infinitive
	(***passé composé***, see *Study Tips*, p. 65)
voudr-	(stem future/conditional
	see *Study Tips*, p. 72)

As you learn more verbs and tenses, you will be able to recognize more patterns and will have to write less on the card.

CHAPTER

17

WHAT IS THE PRESENT TENSE?

The **PRESENT TENSE** indicates that the action is happening at the present time. It can be at the moment the speaker is speaking, a habitual action, or a general truth.

> I *see* you.
> He *smokes* constantly.
> The sun *rises* every day.

IN ENGLISH

There are three forms of the verb that indicate the present tense. Each form has a slightly different meaning:

> Mary *studies* in the library.   PRESENT
> Mary *is studying* in the library.   PRESENT PROGRESSIVE
> Mary *does study* in the library.   PRESENT EMPHATIC

Depending on the way a question is worded, you will automatically choose one of the three above forms in your answer.

> Where does Mary study? She *studies* in the library.
> Where is Mary now? She *is studying* in the library.
> Does Mary study in the library? Yes, she *does [study* in the library].

IN FRENCH

The present tense, **LE PRÉSENT** in French, is a simple tense formed by adding a set of endings to the stem of the verb (see *What is a Verb Conjugation?*, p. 37). Your textbook will give you the present tense endings.

Unlike English, there is only one verb form to indicate the present tense. The French present tense is used to express the meaning of the English present, present progressive, and present emphatic tenses.

> Mary **studies** in the library.
> |
>   étudie

> Mary **is studying** in the library.
>   └──┬──┘
>   étudie

> Mary **does study** in the library.
>   └──┬──┘
>   étudie

CAREFUL — Since the French present tense is always indicated by the ending of the verb, without an auxiliary verb such as *is* and *does,* you must not translate these English auxiliary verbs. Simply put the main verb in the present tense.

40

CHAPTER

18

WHAT IS A PARTICIPLE?

A **PARTICIPLE** is a form of a verb that is used primarily in one of two ways: with an auxiliary verb to indicate certain tenses, or as an adjective to describe something.

> He *has closed* the door.
>
> auxiliary + participle → past tense
>
> He heard me through the *closed* door.
>
> participle describing *door* → adjective

There are two types of participles: the present participle and the past participle.

PRESENT PARTICIPLE

IN ENGLISH

The present participle is easy to recognize because it is the *-ing* form of the verb: *working, studying, dancing, playing.*

The present participle is used primarily as the main verb in compound tenses with the auxiliary verb *to be* (see *What are Auxiliary Verbs?*, p. 44).

> She *is writing* with her new pen.
>
> present progressive of *to write*
>
> They *were sleeping*.
>
> past progressive of *to sleep*

IN FRENCH

The present participle, **LE PARTICIPE PRÉSENT** in French, is formed by adding **-ant** to the stem of the **nous** form of the present tense: chant~~ons~~ → chant**ant** *(singing)*, finiss-~~ons~~ → finiss**ant** *(finishing)*.

The present participle is used differently and less frequently in French than in English. Refer to your textbook.

CAREFUL — Remember that the French equivalent of the English tenses formed with an auxiliary + present participle *(she is singing, they were dancing)* do not use participles in French. These English constructions correspond to a simple tense of the French verb.

*She **is singing**.* $\rightarrow$ Elle **chante**.
present progressive   present (see p. 56)

*They **were dancing**.* $\rightarrow$ Ils **dansaient**.
past progressive   imperfect (see p. 63)

*He **will be staying** here.* $\rightarrow$ Il **restera** ici.
future progressive   future (see p. 70)

PAST PARTICIPLE

IN ENGLISH

The past participle is formed in several ways. It is the form of the verb that follows *I have: I have **spoken**, I have **written**, I have **walked**.*

The past participle has two primary uses:

1. as the main verb in compound tenses with the auxiliary verb *to have*

   I *have **written*** all that I have to say.
   He *has*n't **spoken** to me since our quarrel.

2. as an adjective

   Is the *written* word more important than the *spoken* word?
   describes the noun *word*   describes the noun *word*

IN FRENCH

The past participle, LE PARTICIPE PASSÉ in French, can be regular or irregular. Here are the endings of regular verbs:

- **-er** verbs add **-é** to the stem
- **-ir** verbs add **-i** to the stem
- **-re** verbs add **-u** to the stem

INFINITIVE	STEM	PAST PARTICIPLE
chanter	chant-	chanté
finir	fin-	fini
répondre	répond-	répondu

You will have to memorize irregular past participles individually. As you can see in the examples below, they can be very different from the infinitive.

INFINITIVE	PAST PARTICIPLE
être	été
avoir	eu
lire	lu
comprendre	compris
écrire	écrit

40

50

60

70

80

As in English, the past participle can be used as the main verb of a compound tense or as an adjective.

1. as the main verb in compound tenses with the auxiliary **avoir** *(to have)* or **être** *(to be)*

   Nous avons **compris** la leçon.
   *We have **understood** the lesson.*

   Paul est **allé** à la maison.
   *Paul has **gone** home.*

90 Many tenses are formed with the auxiliary verbs **avoir** or **être** + the past participle of the main verb (see pp. 45-6). These tenses are discussed in various chapters of this handbook.

2. as an adjective that agrees with the noun it modifies in gender and number

   la langue **parlée**
   *the **spoken** language*

   Spoken modifies the noun *language*. Since **la langue** *(language)* is feminine singular, the word for *spoken* must be feminine singular. This is shown by adding an **-e** to **parlé**.

100 les mots **écrits**
   *the **written** words*

   Written modifies the noun *words*. Since **les mots** *(words)* is masculine plural, the word for *written* must be masculine plural. This is shown by adding an **-s** to **écrit**.

WHAT IS THE PAST TENSE?

The PAST TENSE is used to express an action that occurred in
the past.

> I *saw* you yesterday.

IN ENGLISH

There are several verb forms that indicate that the action
took place in the past.[1]

I worked	SIMPLE PAST
I have worked	PRESENT PERFECT
I was working	PAST PROGRESSIVE
I used to work	WITH HELPING VERB USED TO
I did work	PAST EMPHATIC

The simple past is called "simple" because it is a simple
tense; that is, it consists of one word *(worked* in the
example above). The other past tenses are compound
tenses; that is, they consist of more than one word, an
auxiliary plus a main verb *(was working, did work).*

IN FRENCH

There are two French tenses that correspond to all the
English past verbal forms listed above: LE PASSÉ COMPOSÉ
and L'IMPARFAIT. We'll refer to these two tenses by their
French names because their usage does not correspond to
a specific English tense.

LE PASSÉ COMPOSÉ (PRESENT PERFECT)

The **passé composé** is formed with the auxiliary verb **avoir**
(to have) or **être** *(to be)* conjugated in the present tense +
the past participle of the main verb (see *What are Auxiliary
Verbs?*, p. 44 and pp. 59-60 in *What is a Participle?).* As in
English, the past participle does not change form from one
person to another.

> j'ai parlé   *I spoke, I have spoken, I did speak*
> **avoir** past participle
> auxiliary
>
> nous avons parlé   *we spoke, we have spoken, we did speak*

---

[1]A separate section is devoted to the past perfect *(I had worked),* see p. 67.

je suis allé   *I went, I have gone, I did go*

être past participle
auxiliary

il est allé   *he went, he has gone, he did go*

SELECTION OF THE AUXILIARY AVOIR OR ÊTRE

Most verbs use the auxiliary **avoir**. Therefore, it is easier for you to memorize the list of verbs conjugated with **être** and assume that all the other verbs are conjugated with **avoir**.

There are approximately sixteen common verbs, sometimes referred to by grammar books as "verbs of motion," that are conjugated with **être**. "Verbs of motion" is not an accurate description of these verbs since some of them, such as **rester** *(to stay, to remain)*, do not imply motion, and some "verbs of motion," such as **courir** *(to run)*, are conjugated with **avoir**. You will find common "être verbs" easy to memorize in pairs of opposites:

aller	*to go*	≠	venir	*to come*
retourner	*to return*	≠	rester	*to remain*
entrer	*to come in*	≠	sortir	*to go out*
arriver	*to arrive*	≠	partir	*to leave*
monter	*to climb* { ≠		descendre	*to go down*
	≠		tomber	*to fall*
naître	*to be born*	≠	mourir	*to die*

Verbs derived from the above verbs are also conjugated with **être**: **rentrer** *(to return)*, **revenir** *(to come back)*, and **devenir** *(to become)*, among others.

AGREEMENT OF THE PAST PARTICIPLE

The rules of agreement of the past participle depend on whether the auxiliary verb is **avoir** or **être**.

Être — When the auxiliary verb is **être**, the past participle agrees with the subject (review the section *What is a Subject?*, p. 28 and p. 36, lines 179-84).

Pierre **est allé** au cinéma.

subject   past participle
└ masc. sing. (**allé**) ┘
Peter went to the movies.

Marie **est allée** au cinéma.

subject   past participle
└ fem. sing. (**allé + e**) ┘
Mary went to the movies.

80

Paul et Marie **sont allés** au cinéma.

masc. + fem.→ **ils**   past participle
 └ masc. pl. (**allé + s**) ┘

*Paul and Mary **went** to the movies.*

Avoir — When the auxiliary verb is **avoir**, the past participle agrees with the direct object, if the direct object comes before the verb in the sentence (review the section on direct objects, pp. 109-10). If there is no direct object or if the direct object comes after the verb, there is no agreement and the past participle remains in its masculine singular form.

90

Here are a few sentences where the past participle agrees with the direct object because the direct object precedes it.

Le fauteuil qu'il **a acheté** est confortable.
 └ masc. sing. ┘

*The armchair he **bought** is comfortable.*

La chaise qu'il **a achetée** est confortable.
 └ fem. sing. ┘

*The chair he **bought** is comfortable.*

100

Les chaises qu'il **a achetées** sont confortables.
 └ fem. pl. ┘

*The chairs he **bought** are comfortable.*

Le fauteuil et la chaise qu'il **a achetés** sont confortables.

masc. + fem. → **ils**   masc. pl.

*The armchair and the chair he **bought** are comfortable.*

Remember the following when using the **passé composé**:

1. Determine whether the verb takes **avoir** or **être** as the auxiliary.

110

2. Depending on which auxiliary verb is required, apply the appropriate rules of agreement.

L'IMPARFAIT (IMPERFECT)

The **imparfait** is a simple tense formed with the stem of the 1st person plural of the present tense of the verb (see p. 41) + a set of endings **-ais, -ais, -ait, -ions, -iez, -aient**: nous aim~~ons~~ → j'aim**ais** *(I loved)*; nous pren~~ons~~ → il pren**ait** *(he took)*; nous finiss~~ons~~ → ils finiss**aient** *(they finished)*.

120 Two English verb forms indicate that the **imparfait** should be used in French:

1. the verb form includes, or could include, *used to, would*

> As a child, I **used to go** to France every year.
> As a child, I **would go** to France every year.
> Comme enfant, j'**allais** en France chaque année.
> |
> imparfait

2. the verb form is in the past progressive tense

> At 10:00 P.M. last night I **was sleeping**.
> |
> past progressive

130
> A dix heures hier soir je **dormais**.
> |
> imparfait

Except for these two English verb forms, the English verb does not indicate whether you should use the **imparfait** or the **passé composé**.

CAREFUL — The auxiliary *would* does not always correspond to the **imparfait**. When it is part of a contrary-to-fact statement, such as "If I had money, I *would buy* a car," it corre-

140 sponds to the conditional (see *What is the Conditional?*, p. 79).

Selection: LE PASSÉ COMPOSÉ **OR** L'IMPARFAIT

Whether to put a verb in the **passé composé** or the **imparfait** often depends on the context. Here are a few basic guidelines.

- when the English verb can't include *used to, would* (see 1 above) put the French verb in the **passé composé**

> What exercise **did** you **do** last week?
> I **went** to the pool three times last week.

150
> Did do, went cannot be replaced by used to do, used to go.
> Quel exercice **as**-tu **fait** la semaine dernière?
> Je **suis allé** trois fois à la piscine la semaine dernière.
> |___|___|
> passé composé

Compare to:

> What exercise **did** you **do** when you were young?
> I **went** to the pool three times a week.
> Did do, went can be replaced by used to do, used to go.
> Quel exercice **faisais**-tu quand tu **étais** jeune?
> J'**allais** à la piscine trois fois par semaine.
160
> |
> imparfait

▪ when there is more than one action taking place at the same time in the past and you want to indicate what was going on → **imparfait** when something happened → **passé composé**

> *I was reading when he arrived.*
>> The actions "reading" and "arrived" took place at the same time in the past: what was going on? I was reading → **imparfait**; what happened? He arrived → **passé composé**.
>
> Je **lisais** quand il **est arrivé**. 170
>
>   imparfait   passé composé

Compare to:

> *I read, he arrived, then we ate.*
>> The series of actions "read," "arrived" and "ate" happened one after another in the past → **passé composé**.
>
> J'**ai lu**, il **est arrivé**, ensuite nous **avons mangé**.
>
>   passé composé

Sometimes both tenses are possible, but usually one of the two is more logical. Consult your textbook for additional guidelines. 180

STUDY TIPS — THE PASSE COMPOSE

Pattern (see *Tips for Learning Word Forms*, p. 3)
1. Auxiliary Verb (**avoir** or **être**)
   ▪ Some students find it helpful to pair the verbs that take **être** with their opposites so as to remember them more easily (see p. 62).
   ▪ You might also find it helpful to remember that the first letters of the verbs that take **être** spell "Dr. Mrs. Vandertramp."
   > Descendre Rester (Dr)   Monter Retourner Sortir (Mrs)
   > Venir Aller Naître Devenir Entrer Revenir Tomber Rentrer Arriver Mourir Partir (Vandertramp)
2. Main Verb (past participle)
   ▪ Regular past participle: (see p. 59).
   ▪ Irregular past participle: To be learned as vocabulary.

Practice
1. Sort out the verb cards that take **être** as the auxiliary verb.
   ▪ Look at the French side and write or say sentences, putting the verb in the **passé composé**.
   ▪ Look at the English side and repeat the same exercise as above.
2. Sort out the verb cards that take **avoir** as the auxiliary verb. Repeat the two steps under 1 above.

3. Once you've mastered separately the verbs that take **être** as an auxiliary and those that take **avoir**, mix the two piles.

4. Look at the English side and write or say French sentences putting the verb in the **passé composé**. This time you'll have to remember the auxiliary verb and the past participle.

Flashcards

1. Add to each of your verb flashcards the **je** form of the **passé composé**. This will show you whether the verb is conjugated with **avoir** or **être** and will give you the past participle form of the main verb.

prendre	*to take*
j'ai pris	*I took*

2. For reflexive verbs (see p. 129) write the verb in the **passé composé** using "elle" as the subject. This will remind you when the past participle agrees with the reflexive pronoun. Your textbook will explain in detail the **passé composé** of reflexive verbs and the rules of agreement.

Elle s'est lavée.	*She washed (herself).*
Elle s'est lavé les mains.	*She washed her hands.*

WHAT IS THE PAST PERFECT TENSE?

The **PAST PERFECT TENSE**, also called the **PLUPERFECT**, is used to express an action completed in the past before another action or event that also occurred in the past.[1]

She suddenly *remembered* that she *had forgotten* her keys.

simple past   past perfect
1   2

Both actions 1 and 2 occurred in the past, but action 2 preceded action 1. Therefore, action 2 is in the past perfect.

IN ENGLISH

The past perfect is formed with the auxiliary **had** + the past participle of the main verb: *I had walked, he had seen,* etc. In conversation *had* is often shortened to *'d*.

Don't forget that verb tenses indicate the time that an action occurs. Therefore, when verbs in the same sentence are in the same tense, the actions took place at the same time. In order to show that actions took place at different times, different tenses must be used.

Look at the following examples:

The mother *was crying* because her son *was leaving*.

past progressive   past progressive
1   1

Action 1 and action 2 took place at the same time.

The mother *was crying* because her son *had left*.

past progressive   past perfect
1   2

Action 2 took place before action 1.

IN FRENCH

The past perfect, **LE PLUS-QUE-PARFAIT** in French, is formed with the auxiliary verb **avoir** or **être** in the **imparfait** + the past participle of the main verb: **j'avais marché** *(I had walked)*, **elle était allée** *(she had gone)*.

---

[1]You can compare this tense with the future perfect that is used when two actions will happen at different times in the future and you want to stress which action will precede the other (see *What is the Future Perfect Tense?*, p. 73).

The rules of agreement of the past participle are the same as for the **passé composé** (see pp. 62-3).

A verb is put in the **plus-que-parfait** in order to stress that the action of that verb took place before the action of a verb in either the **passé composé** or the **imparfait.**

Observe the sequence of events expressed by the past tenses in the following time-line:

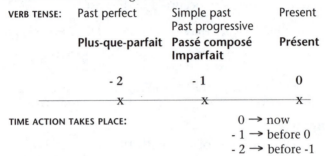

VERB TENSE:	Past perfect	Simple past Past progressive	Present
	Plus-que-parfait	**Passé composé** **Imparfait**	**Présent**
	- 2	- 1	0

TIME ACTION TAKES PLACE:
0 → now
- 1 → before 0
- 2 → before -1

- same verb tense → same moment in time

  *The mother **was crying** because her son **was leaving.***
  La mère **pleurait** parce que son fils **partait.**
         imparfait   imparfait
           -1   -1

  Two actions in the **imparfait** (point -1) show that they took place at the same time in the past (before 0).

- different verb tenses → different times

  *The mother **was crying** because her son **had left.***
  La mère **pleurait** parce que son fils **était parti.**
         imparfait   plus-que-parfait
           -1   -2

  The action in the **plus-que-parfait** (point -2) occurred before the action in the **imparfait** (point -1).

CAREFUL — You cannot always rely on spoken English to determine when to use the past perfect in French. In many cases, English usage permits the use of the simple past to describe an action that preceded another, if it is clear which action came first.

*Mary **forgot** (that) she **saw** that movie.*
    simple past   simple past

*Mary **forgot** (that) she **had seen** that movie.*
    simple past   past perfect

Although the two sentences above mean the same thing, only the sequence of tenses in the second sentence would be correct in French.

Marie **a oublié** qu'elle **avait vu** ce film.

passé composé   **plus-que-parfait**
    -1   -2

The action in the **plus-que-parfait** (point -2) stresses that it was completed before the other action (point -1).

WHAT IS THE FUTURE TENSE?

The **FUTURE TENSE** indicates that an action will take place some time in the future.

> I'll *see* you tomorrow.

IN ENGLISH

The future tense is formed with the auxiliary **will** or **shall** + the dictionary form of the main verb. Note that *shall* is used in formal English (and British English), and *will* in everyday language. In conversation, *shall* and *will* are often shortened to *'ll.*

> Paul and Mary *will do* their homework tomorrow.
> I'*ll leave* tonight.

IN FRENCH

You do not need an auxiliary to show that an action will take place in the future. Future time is indicated by a simple tense formed with a stem, referred to as the **FUTURE STEM,** + endings: **-ai, -as, -a, -ons, -ez, -ont.**

- Future stem of regular verbs:
  -**ir** verbs → infinitive
  -**re** verbs → infinitive without final –**e**
  -**er** verbs → **je** form of the present tense + -**r**

INFINITIVE	FUTURE STEM	
fin**ir**	finir-	*to finish*
répond**re** (répond~~e~~)	répondr-	*to answer*
appel**er** (j'appelle)	appeller-	*to call*

- The future stems of irregular verbs must be learned as vocabulary as they are unpredictable.

INFINITIVE	FUTURE STEM	
aller	ir-	*to go*
venir	viendr-	*to come*
avoir	aur-	*to have*
être	ser-	*to be*

Notice that whatever the stem, regular or irregular, the sound of the letter "r" is always heard before the future endings added to the stem.

CAREFUL — While English uses the present tense after expressions such as *as soon as, when* and *by the time* that introduce an action that will take place in the future, French uses the future tense.

*As soon as he **returns**, I **will call**.*
          present   future

Dès qu'il **reviendra**, je **téléphonerai**.
         future   future

"as soon as he *will come* . . ."

*She **will come** when she **is** ready.*
       future   present

Elle **viendra** quand elle **sera** prête.
      future   future

". . . when she *will be* ready"

French is stricter than English in its use of tenses.

THE IMMEDIATE FUTURE

In English and in French an action that will occur some time in the near future can also be expressed without using the future tense itself, but with a construction that implies the future. This construction is called the **IMMEDIATE FUTURE**.

IN ENGLISH

The immediate future is expressed with the verb ***to go*** in the present progressive tense + the infinitive of the main verb: *I am going to walk, she is going to see*, etc.

            similar meaning

*I am going **to sing**.*   *I will sing.*
present progressive   future tense
of *to go* + infinitive

IN FRENCH

The same construction exists in French. It is called **LE FUTUR IMMÉDIAT** or **LE FUTUR PROCHE** because the future action is considered nearer at hand than an action expressed by a verb in the future tense.

The immediate future is formed with the verb **aller** *(to go)* in the present tense + the infinitive of the main verb: **je vais marcher** *(I'm going to walk)*, **elle va voir** *(she's going to see)*.

Look at the difference between the forms of the immediate future and the future tense.

80

Je **vais chanter.**   Je **chanterai.**

present of **aller** + infinitive   future tense
immediate future

I am going to sing.   *I will sing.*

present of *to go* + infinitive   future tense
immediate future

In conversational French, the immediate future often replaces the future tense.

STUDY TIPS — THE FUTURE TENSE

Pattern (see *Tips for Learning Vocabulary*, p. 1)
1 Future stems (see p. 70)
2. Endings (see your textbook and *Study Tips — Verb conjugations*, p. 42)
- The 1st, 2nd, and 3rd persons singular, as well as the 3rd person plural, are identical to the same persons of the present tense of the verb **avoir**: **–ai, –as, –a,** and **–ont.**
- The 1st and 2nd persons plural are identical to endings of the same persons of the present tense of most verbs: **–ons** and **–ez.**

Flashcards

On your verb cards add the irregular future stem, if there is one. Note: the future stem will also be the stem for the conditional (see *What is the Conditional?*, p. 79).

vouloir   *to want*
voudr-   *(stem: future/conditional)*

Practice

1. Sort out the verbs with regular future stems.
   - Look at the French side. Write (on a separate sheet of paper) or say sentences putting the verb in the future tense.
   - Look at the English side. Write (on a separate sheet of paper) or say French sentences putting the verb in the future tense.
2. Sort out the verbs with irregular future stems. Repeat the two steps under 1 above.
3. Mix the pile of verbs with regular and irregular future stems. Repeat the two steps under 1 above.

WHAT IS THE FUTURE PERFECT TENSE?

The FUTURE PERFECT TENSE is used to express an action that will   1
occur before another action in the future or before a specific
time in the future.[1]

> By the time we leave, he *will have finished.*
>
>   future event   future perfect
>   2   1

Both actions 1 and 2 will occur at some future time, but action
1 will be completed before action 2 takes place. Therefore,
action 1 is in the future perfect tense.

> I won't meet him. I *will have left* before he arrives.   10
>
>   future perfect   future event
>   1   2

Both action 1 and event 2 will occur at some future time, but
action 1 will be completed before a specific event in the future.
Therefore, action 1 is in the future perfect tense.

IN ENGLISH

The future perfect is formed with the auxiliary **will have** +
the past participle of the main verb: *I will have walked, she
will have gone.* In conversation *will* is often shortened   20
to *'ll.*

The future perfect is often used following expressions such
as *by then, by that time, by* + a date.

> By the end of the month, he*'ll have graduated.*
> By June, I*'ll have saved* enough to buy a car.

IN FRENCH

The future perfect, LE FUTUR ANTÉRIEUR in French, is formed
with the auxiliary **avoir** or **être** in the future tense + the
past participle of the main verb: **j'aurai marché** *(I'll have*   30
walked), **elle sera allée** *(she'll have gone).*

The rules of agreement of the past participle are the
same as for the **passé composé** (see pp. 62-3).

---

[1]You can compare this tense to the past perfect that is used when two actions occurred
at different times in the past and you want to stress which action preceded the other
(see *What is the Past Perfect Tense?*, p. 67).

As in English, a verb is put in the **futur antérieur** tense in order to stress that the action of that verb will take place before the action of a verb in the future, or before a specific future time.

Observe the sequence of events expressed by the future tenses in the following time-line:

VERB TENSE:	**Present**	**Future perfect**	**Future**
	Présent	Futur antérieur	Futur
	0	**1**	**2**

———X————————X————————X—

TIME ACTION TAKES PLACE: 0 → now
                                        1 → after 0 and before 2
                                        2 → after 0

*When I've **learned** French, I'll go to Paris.*
Quand j'**aurai appris** le français, j'**irai** à Paris.

          1   2

The action in the **futur antérieur** (point 1) will occur before the action in the **futur** (point 2).

*Before school starts, I'll **have left**.*
Avant la rentrée des classes, je **serai parti**.

               2   1

The action in the **futur antérieur** (point 1) will occur before the future event (point 2).

CAREFUL — While English uses the present tense after conjunctions such as *when* (**quand**) and *as soon as* (**dès que**), French uses the **futur antérieur**.

*When he **finishes** this course, he'**ll understand** French.*
     present   future
Quand il **aura fini** ce cours, il **comprendra** le français.

Consult your textbook for other uses of the **futur antérieur**.

WHAT IS MEANT BY MOOD?

MOOD in the grammatical sense is a term applied to verb tenses.

Different moods serve different purposes. For instance, verb tenses that state a fact belong to one mood *(you are studying, you studied)* and the verb tense that gives orders belongs to another *(Study!)*. Some moods have multiple tenses, others have only one tense.

You should recognize the names of moods so that you will know what your French textbook is referring to when it uses these terms. You will learn when to use the various moods as you learn verbs and their tenses.

IN ENGLISH

Verbs can be in one of four moods:

1. The **INDICATIVE MOOD** is used to state the action of the verb; that is, to *indicate* facts. This is the most common mood and most of the verb forms that you use in everyday conversation belong to the indicative mood. The majority of the tenses studied in this handbook belong to the indicative mood: for instance, the present tense (see p. 56), the past tense (see p. 61), and the future tense (p. 70).

> Paul *studies* French.
> present indicative

> Mary *was* here.
> past indicative

> They *will come* tomorrow.
> future indicative

2. The **IMPERATIVE MOOD** is used to give commands or orders (see *What is the Imperative?*, p. 77). This mood is not divided into tenses.

> Paul, *study* French now!
> Mary, *be* home on time!

3. The SUBJUNCTIVE MOOD is used to express an attitude or feeling toward the action of the verb; it is *subjective* about it (see *What is the Subjunctive?*, p. 83). In English, this mood is not divided into tenses.

> The school requires that students *study* French.
> I wish that Mary *were* here.
> The teacher recommends that he *do* his homework.

4. The CONDITIONAL MOOD is primarily used to express: 1. a wish or desire more politely and 2. a hypothetical state of affairs or an event which can only be realized if another event occurs. It has two tenses: the present conditional and the past conditional (see *What is the Conditional?*, p. 79).

> *Would* you *close* the door.
> He *would go* to France if he had the money.

IN FRENCH

Verbs can be in one of four moods.

1. As in English, the INDICATIVE MOOD is the most common and most of the tenses you will learn belong to this mood.

2. As in English, the IMPERATIVE MOOD is used to give orders and it is not divided into tenses.

3. Unlike English, however, the SUBJUNCTIVE MOOD is used very frequently. It has two main tenses: the present subjunctive and the past subjunctive. Textbooks use the term "present subjunctive" to distinguish it from the "present indicative" and the "present conditional."

4. As in English, the CONDITIONAL MOOD has two tenses: the present conditional and the past conditional. Textbooks use the term "present conditional" to distinguish it from the "present indicative" and "present subjunctive."

When there is no reference to mood, the tense belongs to the most common mood, the indicative.

WHAT IS THE IMPERATIVE?

The IMPERATIVE is used to give someone an order. The AFFIRMA-TIVE IMPERATIVE is an order to do something. The NEGATIVE IMPERATIVE is an order not to do something. [1]

> *Come* here!
> *Don't come* here!

IN ENGLISH

There are two types of command, depending on who is told to do, or not to do, something.

1. **"YOU" COMMAND** — When an order is given to one or more persons, the present tense minus the subject pro- [10] noun *you* is used.

AFFIRMATIVE IMPERATIVE	NEGATIVE IMPERATIVE
Answer the phone.	*Don't answer* the phone.
Clean your room.	*Don't clean* your room.
Speak softly.	*Don't speak* softly.

2. **"WE" COMMAND** — When an order is given to oneself as well as to others, the phrase *let's* (a contraction of *let us*) is used + the dictionary form of the verb.

AFFIRMATIVE IMPERATIVE	NEGATIVE IMPERATIVE
Let's leave.	*Let's not leave.*	[20]
Let's go to the movies.	*Let's not go* to the movies.

IN FRENCH

As in English, there are affirmative and negative com-mands. However, there are three forms because the sin-gular *you* command has both a familiar and a formal form.

To form the imperative, most verbs use the present tense minus the subject pronoun. Your textbook will go over the verbs that have an irregular imperative.

1. **"TU" COMMAND** — When an order is given to a person to [30] whom one says **tu**, the 2nd person singular of present tense is used minus the subject pronoun **tu**.

AFFIRMATIVE IMPERATIVE	NEGATIVE IMPERATIVE
Viens.	Ne viens pas.
Come.	*Don't come.*
Prends le livre.	Ne prends pas le livre.
Take the book.	*Don't take the book.*

Note that in the imperative **-er** verbs drop the final "-s" in the **tu**-form:

PRESENT TENSE	IMPERATIVE
tu manges	Mange!
you eat	*Eat!*
tu ne chantes **pas**	Ne **chante** pas!
you don't sing	*Don't sing!*

2. **"Vous" COMMAND** — When an order is given to a person to whom one says **vous,** or to more than one person, the 2nd person plural of the present tense is used minus the subject pronoun **vous**.

AFFIRMATIVE IMPERATIVE	NEGATIVE IMPERATIVE
Venez.	**Ne venez pas.**
Come.	*Don't come.*
Prenez le livre.	**Ne prenez pas** le livre.
Take the book.	*Don't take the book.*

3. **"Nous" COMMAND** — When an order is given to oneself as well as to others, the 1st person plural of the present tense is used minus the subject pronoun **nous**.

AFFIRMATIVE IMPERATIVE	NEGATIVE IMPERATIVE
Allons.	**N'allons pas.**
Let's go.	*Let's not go.*
Prenons le livre.	**Ne prenons pas** le livre.
Let's take the book.	*Let's not take the book.*

In English and in French the absence of the subject pronoun in the sentence is a good indication that you are dealing with an imperative and not a present tense (see *What is the Present Tense?,* p. 56).

Vous répondez au téléphone.
You answer the phone.
|
present

Répondez au téléphone.
Answer the phone.
|
imperative

WHAT IS THE CONDITIONAL?

The **CONDITIONAL** is a mood that gets its name because its [1]
tenses are primarily used in sentences that imply a condition
or that state a hypothesis.

> If I were offered the job, I *would take* it.
>
>   condition   verb in the conditional

The conditional mood has a present and past tense (see
What is Meant by Mood?, p. 75).

PRESENT CONDITIONAL

IN ENGLISH

The present conditional is made up of two words: the aux- [10]
iliary **would** + the dictionary form of the main verb:
I would eat, they would talk, we would go.

The present conditional is used in the following ways:

1. as a polite form with *like* and in polite requests

> I *would like* to eat.
>> More polite than "I want to eat."

> *Would* you please close the door.
>> "Please close the door" is softened by the use of *would*.

2. in the result clause of **HYPOTHETICAL CONTRARY-TO-FACT** [20]
STATEMENTS

A **CLAUSE** is a part of a sentence composed of a group of
words containing a subject and a verb. Contrary-to-fact
statements include two clauses: 1. the *IF*-**CLAUSE** that
states a condition that is not met and 2. the **RESULT**
CLAUSE that states what could result if and when the
condition were ever fulfilled.

>   *if*-clause   result clause
>
> If Paul had money, he *would buy* a car. [30]
>
> subject verb   subject   verb
>   past   present conditional

When the condition is not met at the present time but
could be met in the future (Paul did not have money at
the time, but could have money in the future), the verb
of the *if*-clause is in the past tense and the verb of the
result clause is in the present conditional.

IN FRENCH

Unlike English, you do not need an auxiliary to indicate the present conditional, LE CONDITIONNEL PRÉSENT in French. It is a simple tense formed with the future stem (see p. 70) + the imperfect endings (p. 63): je parler**ais** (*I would speak*), il finir**ait** (*he would finish*), nous vendr**ions** (*we would sell*).

The present conditional is used in the same ways as in English:

1. as a polite form or in polite requests

Je **voudrais** un sandwich.

present conditional
*I **would like** a sandwich.*

Pourriez-vous fermer la porte?

present conditional
***Would you please** close the door?*

2. in the result clause of a contrary-to-fact statements

As in English, contrary-to-fact statements have two clauses: 1. the *SI*-CLAUSE that starts with **si** (**s'** before a vowel) and 2. the RESULT CLAUSE.

When the condition is not met at the present time, but could be met in the future, the verb of the **si**-clause is in the **imparfait** and the verb of the result clause is in the **conditionnel présent**.

Si Paul avait de l'argent, il **achèterait** une voiture.

imparfait   conditionnel présent
*If Paul had money, he **would buy** a car.*

CAREFUL — The auxiliary *would* does not correspond to the French conditional when it stands for *used to*, as in "she *would talk* while he painted." In this sentence, it means *used to talk* and requires the imperfect (see p. 64).

PAST CONDITIONAL

IN ENGLISH

The past conditional is made up of the auxiliary ***would have*** + the past participle of the main verb (see p. 59): *I would have eaten, they would have talked, we would have gone.* In conversation *would have* is often shortened to *would've*.

When the condition was not met in the past, the verb of the *if*-clause clause is in the past perfect tense (see p. 67) and the verb of the result clause is in the past conditional.

```
        if-clause                    result clause
      ┌──────────┐              ┌──────────────────┐
      If Paul had had money, he would have bought a car.
          └───┬───┘                  └──────┬──────┘
          past perfect              past conditional
```

The condition was contrary-to-fact in the past (Paul did not have money) and, therefore, he was unable to buy a car.

IN FRENCH

The past conditional, LE CONDITIONNEL PASSÉ in French, is formed with the auxiliary **avoir** or **être** in the present conditional + the past participle of the main verb: **j'aurais mangé** *(I would have eaten)*, **elle serait allée** *(she would have gone)*. The same rules of agreement apply as for the **passé composé**, see pp. 62-3.

When the condition was not met in the past, the verb of the **si**-clause is in the **plus-que-parfait** and the verb of the result clause is in the **conditionnel passé**.

```
    Si Paul avait eu de l'argent, il aurait acheté une voiture.
          └────┬────┘                   └──────┬──────┘
        plus-que-parfait              conditionnel passé
```
*If Paul had had money, he **would have bought** a car.*

IF-CLAUSES SEQUENCE OF TENSES

In English and in French the *if*-clause can come before or after the result clause and the tense of one clause depends on the tense of the other.

- condition may be met at any time

IF-CLAUSE	←→	RESULT CLAUSE
present		future
présent		**futur**

```
    If he studies, he will pass.
         │            └───┬───┘
       present         future
    S'il étudie, il réussira.
         │             │
      présent        futur
```

- condition is contrary-to-fact at the present time, but could be met in the future

IF-CLAUSE	←→	RESULT CLAUSE
simple past		present conditional
imparfait		**conditionnel présent**

```
    If he studied, he would pass.
         │             └────┬────┘
      simple past    present conditional
    S'il étudiait, il réussirait.
         │              │
      imparfait    conditionnel présent
```

- condition was contrary-to-fact in the past

IF-CLAUSE ←→	RESULT CLAUSE
past perfect	past conditional
plus-que-parfait	**conditionnel passé**

*If he **had studied**, he **would have passed**.*

     past perfect   past conditional

S'il **avait étudié**, il **aurait réussi**.

     plus-que-parfait   conditionnel passé

CAREFUL — In English and in French, the tense of the verb is tied to the type of clause: 1. the conditional is only used in the result clause 2. the conditional is only used in the result clause when the *if*-clause is contrary-to-fact. In the three examples above, there would be no change of tense in each clause if the result clause had preceded the "if-clause."

USE OF THE CONDITIONAL IN INDIRECT SPEECH

DIRECT SPEECH is a word-for-word quotation of what someone said as opposed to **INDIRECT SPEECH** that repeats or reports someone's words. In written form a direct statement is always between quotation marks.

In both English and French, the conditional is used in the reported statement.

IN ENGLISH

Here is an example of a direct statement changed to an indirect statement.

DIRECT STATEMENT   Paul said: *"Mary will arrive this evening."*

       1   2
      past   future

INDIRECT STATEMENT   Paul said *Mary would arrive this evening.*

       1   2
      past   present conditional

In the direct statement, action 2 is merely a quotation in the future tense. In the indirect statement, action 2 *(Mary would come)* is called a **FUTURE-IN-THE-PAST** because it takes place after another action in the past *(Paul said)*.

IN FRENCH

As in English, the conditional is used in the reported statement to express a future-in-the-past.

Paul a dit que Marie **viendrait ce soir.**

       present conditional

*Paul said (that) Mary **would arrive** this evening.*

WHAT IS THE SUBJUNCTIVE?

The SUBJUNCTIVE is a mood used to express a wish, hope, uncertainty or other similar attitude toward a fact or an idea. 1

I wish he *were* here.
| |
subject's subjunctive
wish

The teacher insisted that the homework *be* neat.
       | |
     subject's   subjunctive
     feelings

IN ENGLISH
10
The subjunctive verb form is difficult to recognize because it is spelled like other tenses of the verb: the dictionary form and the simple past tense.

INDICATIVE	SUBJUNCTIVE
He *writes* a lot.	The course requires that he *write* a lot.
indicative present *to write*	subjunctive (same as dictionary form)
I *am* in Paris.	I wish I *were* in Paris.
indicative present *to be*	subjunctive (same as past tense)

20
The subjunctive is used in very few constructions. Besides the few examples above, it is used primarily in expressions such as: "Long *live* the Republic!" "God *save* the Queen!"

IN FRENCH

The subjunctive is used very frequently; unfortunately English usage will rarely help you decide when to use it in French. Here are a few suggestions as to how to approach the subjunctive when it is introduced in your textbook.

1. When you learn the conjugation of verbs in the present tense of the subjunctive, it is useful to compare those forms to the present indicative. This will help you to remember what distinguishes one from the other. 30

2. Learn the verbs and expressions that require the subjunctive for the verb in the dependent clause. Consult your textbook for the rules that apply when these verbs and expressions are not followed by a dependent clause.

Here are a few examples. Notice that each clause has a different subject and that the French dependent clauses start with the subordinating conjunction **que** *(that)*.

- verbs of will or desire

Je veux que **tu sois** sage.

vouloir   être
indicative   subjunctive

I want you to be good.
(word-for-word: "*I want that you be good*")

Elle préfère que **je lise** ce livre en français.

préférer   lire
indicative   subjunctive

She prefers that I read that book in French.

- expressions of necessity

Il faut que **j'apprenne** le français.

falloir   apprendre
indicative subjunctive

It is necessary that I learn French.

- verbs of doubt

Je doute que **Marie sache** parler français.

douter   savoir
indicative   subjunctive

I doubt (that) Mary knows how to speak French.

- expressions of emotion

Les enfants sont heureux que **vous veniez** ce soir.

être   venir
indicative   subjunctive

The children are happy (that) you are coming this evening.

- expressions of opinion

Il est dommage qu'**elle soit** malade.

regretter   être
indicative   subjunctive

It is too bad (that) she is sick.

Notice that the French expressions don't always have a word-for-word English equivalent.

Since English structures are not relevant, we refer you to your textbook regarding the use of the subjunctive in French.

WHAT IS AN ADJECTIVE?

An ADJECTIVE is a word that describes a noun or a pronoun. There are different types of adjectives that are classified according to the way they describe a noun or pronoun.

DESCRIPTIVE ADJECTIVE — A descriptive adjective indicates a quality; it tells what kind of noun it is (see p. 86).

> She read an *interesting* book.
> He has *brown* eyes.

POSSESSIVE ADJECTIVE— A possessive adjective shows possession; it tells whose noun it is (see p. 92).

> *His* book is lost.
> *Our* parents are away.

INTERROGATIVE ADJECTIVE — An interrogative adjective asks a question about a noun (see p. 97).

> *What* book is lost?
> *Which* parents did you speak to?

DEMONSTRATIVE ADJECTIVE — A demonstrative adjective points out a noun (see p. 99).

> *This* teacher is excellent.
> *That* question is very appropriate.

IN ENGLISH

English adjectives usually do not change their form, regardless of the noun or pronoun described.

IN FRENCH

The principal difference between English and French adjectives is that while in English adjectives do not change their form, in French adjectives change in order to agree in gender and number with the noun or pronoun they modify.

STUDY TIPS — DESCRIPTIVE ADJECTIVES (SEE P. 88)

STUDY TIPS — POSSESSIVE ADJECTIVES (SEE P. 96)

CHAPTER

28

WHAT IS A DESCRIPTIVE ADJECTIVE?

A **DESCRIPTIVE ADJECTIVE** is a word that indicates a quality of a noun or pronoun. As the name implies, it *describes* the noun or pronoun.

> The book is *interesting.*
> noun   descriptive
> described adjective

IN ENGLISH

A descriptive adjective does not change form, regardless of the noun or pronoun it modifies.

> The students are *intelligent.*
> She is an *intelligent* person.
>
> > The adjective *intelligent* is the same although the persons described are different in number *(students* is plural and *person* is singular).

IN FRENCH

While English descriptive adjectives never change form, French descriptive adjectives change form in order to agree in gender and number with the noun or pronoun they modify.

Most adjectives add an "**-e**" to the masculine form to make the feminine form and an "**-s**" to the masculine singular or the feminine singular form to make it plural.

*The book is **blue.***	Le livre est **bleu.**
	masc. masc.
	sing. sing.
*The dress is **blue.***	La robe est **bleue.**
	fem. fem. (**bleu + e**)
	sing. sing.
*The books are **blue.***	Les livres sont **bleus.**
	masc. masc. (**bleu + s**)
	pl. pl.
*The dresses are **blue.***	Les robes sont **bleues.**
	fem. fem. (**bleu + es**)
	pl. pl.

ATTRIBUTIVE AND PREDICATE ADJECTIVES
IN ENGLISH

Descriptive adjectives are divided into two groups depending on how they are connected to the noun they modify. [40]

1. A **PREDICATE ADJECTIVE** is connected to the noun it modifies, always the subject of the sentence, by **LINKING VERBS** such as *to be, to feel, to look.*

> The children are *good.*
> noun | linking | predicate
> described | verb | adjective

> The house looks *small.*
> noun | linking | predicate [50]
> described | verb | adjective

2. An **ATTRIBUTIVE ADJECTIVE** is connected directly to the noun it modifies and always precedes it.

> The *good* children were praised.
> attributive | noun
> adjective | described

> The family lives in a *small* house.
> attributive | noun
> adjective | described [60]

IN FRENCH

As in English, descriptive adjectives can be identified as predicate or attributive adjectives, depending on how they are connected to the noun they modify. As in English, French predicate adjectives are placed after linking verbs such as **être** *(to be)* and follow the same word order.

While English attributive descriptive adjectives always come before the noun they modify, most, but not all, French attributive descriptive adjectives come after the [70] noun they modify.

> Elle lit un **livre intéressant**.
> *She is reading an **interesting book**.*

However, some common French descriptive adjectives, come before the noun they modify.

> Jean est un **beau garçon** et Marie est une **jolie fille**.
> *John is a **handsome boy** and Mary is a **pretty girl**.*

Your textbook will tell you, and you will have to learn, which French descriptive adjectives precede and which follow the noun they modify.

STUDY TIPS — DESCRIPTIVE ADJECTIVES

Flashcards (see *Tips for Learning Vocabulary*, p. 1)
1. Create flashcards indicating the adjective twice on the French side, once modifying a masculine noun and once modifying a feminine noun. This will show you the masculine and feminine forms of the adjective and whether it is placed before or after the noun it modifies. (Refer to your textbook for the placement of adjectives in a sentence.)

un stylo vert	*a green pen*
une robe verte	*a green dress*
un vieux livre	*an old book*
une vieille robe	*an old dress*

2. If the adjective has irregular singular or plural forms, illustrate them.

le beau jardin	*the beautiful garden*
les beaux jardins	*the beautiful gardens*
le bel appartement	*the beautiful apartment*
les beaux appartements	*the beautiful apartments*
la belle maison	*the beautiful house*

Practice
Write short sentences using the descriptive adjectives you learned, concentrating on the descriptive adjectives with irregular forms.

WHAT IS MEANT BY COMPARISON OF ADJECTIVES?

The term **COMPARISON OF ADJECTIVES** is used when two or more persons or things have the same quality indicated by a descriptive adjective and we want to show which of these persons or things has a greater, lesser, or equal degree of that quality.

comparison of adjectives

Paul is *tall* but Mary is *taller*.

adjective
modifies *Paul*

adjective
modifies *Mary*

Both nouns, Paul and Mary, have the same quality indicated by the adjective *tall,* and we want to show that Mary has a greater degree of that quality (i.e., she is *taller* than Paul).

In English and in French there are two types of comparison: comparative and superlative.

COMPARATIVE
The comparative compares a quality of a person or thing with the same quality in another person or thing. The comparison can indicate that one or the other has more, less, or the same amount of that quality.

IN ENGLISH
Let's go over the three degrees of comparison:

1. The comparison of **GREATEST DEGREE** (more) is formed differently depending on the length of the adjective being compared.

   ▪ short adjective + *-er* + *than*

   Paul is tall*er than* Mary.
   She is smart*er than* her sister.

   ▪ *more* + longer adjective + *than*

   Paul is *more* intelligent *than* his brother.
   His car is *more* expensive *than* ours.

2. The comparison of **LESSER DEGREE** (less) is formed as follows: *not as* + adjective + *as,* or *less* + adjective + *than*.

Mary is *not as* tall *as* Paul.
My car is *less* expensive *than* your car.

3. The comparison of **EQUAL DEGREE** (same) is formed as follows: *as* + adjective + *as*.

Paul is *as* tall *as* Mary.
My car is *as* expensive *as* yours.

IN FRENCH

There are the same three degrees of comparison of adjectives as in English.

Like all French adjectives, French comparative adjectives agree with the noun they modify. In the case of comparative adjectives that describe more than one noun, they agree in gender and number with the subject.

1. The comparison of **GREATER DEGREE** is formed as follows: **plus** *(more)* + adjective + **que** *(than)*.

Paul est **plus** actif **que** Marie.

masc. sing. agrees with subject → Paul
*Paul is **more** active **than** Mary.*

2. The comparison of **LESSER DEGREE** is formed as follows: **moins** *(less)* + adjective + **que** *(than)*.

Marie est **moins** active **que** Paul.

fem. sing. agrees with subject → Marie
*Mary is **less** active **than** Paul.*

3. The comparison of **EQUAL DEGREE** is formed as follows: **aussi** *(as)* + adjective + **que** *(as)*.

Marie est **aussi** active **que** Paul.
*Mary is **as** active **as** Paul.*

SUPERLATIVE

The superlative is used to stress the highest and lowest degrees of a quality.

IN ENGLISH

Let's go over the two degrees of the superlative:

1. The superlative of **GREATEST DEGREE** is formed differently depending on the length of the adjective.

 ▪ *the* + short adjective + *-est*

 Mary is *the* smart*est*.
 My car is *the* cheap*est* on the market.

■ *the most* + long adjective

Mary is *the most* intelligent.
His car is *the most* expensive.

2. The superlative of LOWEST DEGREE is formed as follows: *the least* + adjective.

Paul is *the least* active.
His car is *the least* expensive.

IN FRENCH

There are the same two degrees of the superlative as in English.

1. The superlative of GREATEST DEGREE is formed as follows: **le, la** or **les** (depending on the gender and number of the noun described) + **plus** *(most)* + adjective.

Marie est **la plus** active de la famille.
       fem. sing.
*Mary is **the most active** in the family.*

Paul est **le plus** grand.
       masc. sing.
*Paul is **the tallest**.*

Marie et Paul sont **les plus** intelligents de la classe.
       masc. pl. (see p. 36)
*Mary and Paul are **the most intelligent** in the class.*

2. The superlative of LOWEST DEGREE is formed as follows: **le, la** or **les** (depending on the gender and number of the noun described) + **moins** *(less)* + adjective.

Paul est **le moins actif** de la classe.
       masc. sing.
*Paul is **the least active** in the class.*

CAREFUL — In English and in French, a few adjectives have irregular forms of comparison that you will have to memorize individually.

ADJECTIVE	Cette pomme est **bonne**. *This apple is **good**.*
COMPARATIVE	Cette pomme est **meilleure**. *This apple is **better**.*
SUPERLATIVE	Cette pomme est **la meilleure**. *This apple is **the best**.*

CHAPTER

30

WHAT IS A POSSESSIVE ADJECTIVE?

A **POSSESSIVE ADJECTIVE** is a word that describes a noun by showing who possesses that noun.

> Whose house is that? It's *my* house.
>
> > *My* shows who possesses the noun *house*. The possessor is "me." The object possessed is *house*.

IN ENGLISH

Like subject pronouns, possessive adjectives are identified according to the person they represent (see p. 32).

SINGULAR POSSESSOR

1ST PERSON		my
2ND PERSON		your
3RD PERSON	MASCULINE	his
	FEMININE	her
	NEUTER	its

PLURAL POSSESSOR

1ST PERSON	our
2ND PERSON	your
3RD PERSON	their

A possessive adjective changes according to the possessor, regardless of the noun possessed.

> Is that John's house? Yes, it is *his* house.
> Is that Mary's house? Yes, it is *her* house.
>
> > Although the object possessed is the same *(house)*, different possessive adjectives *(his* and *her)* are used because the possessors are different *(John* and *Mary)*.

> Is that John's house? Yes, it is *his* house.
> Are those John's keys? Yes, they are *his* keys.
>
> > Although the objects possessed are different *(house* and *keys)*, the same possessive adjective *(his)* is used because the possessor is the same *(John)*.

IN FRENCH

Like English, a French possessive adjective changes according to the possessor, but unlike English it also agrees, like all French adjectives, in gender and number with the noun possessed.

For example, in the phrase **mon frère** *(my brother)* the 1ˢᵗ person singular possessor *(my)* is indicated by the first letter of the possessive adjective, **m-**, and the gender and number of the noun possessed, **frère** *(brother)*, that is masculine singular, is reflected in the masculine singular ending -**on**.

Let us see what happens when we change *my brother* to *my sister.*

> *I love **my sister.***
> J'aime **ma sœur.**
>
> | fem. sing. ending
> 1ˢᵗ pers. sing. possessor

> The first letter **m-** remains the same because the possessor is still the 1ˢᵗ person, but the ending changes to -**a** to agree with **sœur** *(sister)* that is feminine singular.

The pattern of possessive adjectives for a singular possessor is different from the pattern of possessive adjectives for a plural possessor. We have the divided the French possessive adjectives into these two groups.

SINGULAR POSSESSOR (1ˢᵗ, 2ᴺᴰ AND 3ᴿᴰ PERS. SING.)
my, your (tu-form), his, her, its

In French, each of these possessive adjectives has three forms depending on the gender and number of the noun possessed: the masculine singular, the feminine singular, and the plural (the same for both genders).

To choose the correct possessive adjective:

1. Indicate the possessor with the first letter of the possessive adjective.

my	**m-**
your	**t-** (**tu**-form)
his	
her	} **s-**
its	

2. Choose the ending according to the gender and number of the noun possessed.

- noun possessed is masculine singular (or feminine singular beginning with a vowel) → add -**on**

Anne lit **mon** livre.	*Ann reads **my** book.*
masc. sing.	noun possessed
Anne lit **ton** livre.	*Ann reads **your** book.*
Anne lit **son** livre.	*Ann reads **her** (**his**) book.*

Paul connaît **mon** amie.   *Paul knows **my** friend.*
         | |
   fem. sing.   noun possessed
 begins with vowel
Paul connaît **ton** amie.   *Paul knows **your** friend.*
Paul connaît **son** amie.   *Paul knows **his (her)** friend.*

- noun possessed is feminine singular beginning with a consonant → add -**a**

Paul lit **ma** lettre.   *Paul reads **my** letter.*
         | |
     fem. sing.   noun possessed
Paul lit **ta** lettre.   *Paul reads **your** letter.*
Paul lit **sa** lettre.   *Paul reads **his (her)** letter.*

- noun possessed is plural → add -**es**

Anne lit **mes** livres.   *Ann reads **my** books.*
          | |
      masc. pl.   noun possessed

Paul lit **tes** lettres.   *Paul reads **your** letters.*
          |
      fem. pl.

Elle lit **ses** livres.   *She is reading **his (her)** books.*
          |
      masc. pl.

3. Select the proper form according to the two steps above.

Let us apply the above steps to examples:

   *Paul is looking at **his** mother.*
      1. Possessor: *his* → 3ʳᵈ pers. sing. → s-
      2. Noun possessed: **Mère** *(mother)* is feminine singular → **a**
      3. Selection: **s-** + -**a**
   Paul regarde **sa** mère.

   *Paul is looking at **his** father.*
      1. Possessor: *his* → 3ʳᵈ pers. sing. → s-
      2. Noun possessed: **Père** *(father)* is masculine singular → **on**
      3. Selection: **s-** + -**on**
   Paul regarde **son** père.

CAREFUL — Make sure that the ending of the possessive adjective agrees with the noun it modifies and not with the possessor.

PLURAL POSSESSOR (1ˢᵀ, 2ᴺᴰ AND 3ᴿᴰ PERS. PL.)
our, your (vous-form), **their**

In French, each of these possessive adjectives has only two forms depending on the number of the noun possessed; that is, whether the noun possessed is singular or plural.

- noun possessed is singular → **notre, votre,** or **leur**

Marie est **notre** fille. | *Mary is **our** daughter.*

    noun possessed singular

Paul lit **votre** lettre. | *Paul reads **your** letter.*
Ils lisent **leur** lettre. | *They read **their** letter.*

- noun possessed is plural → **nos, vos,** or **leurs**

Les parents sont **nos** amis. | *The parents are **our** friends.*

    noun possessed plural

Anne lit **vos** livres. | *Ann reads **your** books.*
Elles lisent **leurs** lettres. | *They read **their** letters.*

Although **votre,** and **vos** are classified as "the second person plural," they can refer to just one person when used as a formal form of address (see pp. 33-4).

CAREFUL — Make sure that you use the same "you" form, either familiar or formal, for the verb and the possessive adjective: *"You* are reading *your* letter" would be either "**Tu** lis **ta** lettre" or "**Vous** lisez **votre** lettre."

SUMMARY

Here is a chart you can use as a reference.

POSSESSOR SINGULAR		NOUN POSSESSED	
		SINGULAR	PLURAL
my	MASC.	mon	
	FEM. + VOWEL	mon	mes
	FEM.	ma	
your (*tu* form)	MASC.	ton	
	FEM. + VOWEL	ton	tes
	FEM.	ta	
his, her, its	MASC.	son	
	FEM. + VOWEL	son	ses
	FEM.	sa	
POSSESSOR PLURAL		NOUN POSSESSED	
		SINGULAR	PLURAL
our		notre	nos
your (*vous* form)		votre	vos
their		leur	leurs

Pattern (see Tips *For Learning Word Forms*, p. 3)
It will be easy for you to establish a pattern if you follow our instructions under "Singular Possessor" and "Plural Possessor" (pp. 93-5).

Practice

1. Sort out your noun flashcards and select a few of the following:
   - masculine nouns and feminine nouns beginning with a consonant
   - masculine nouns and feminine nouns beginning with a vowel

2. Look at the French side and go through the cards saying the noun preceded by the correct forms of the possessive adjective. Concentrate on the singular forms **mon, ton, son** since they are the forms that change.

le jardin	*garden*
mon jardin, ton jardin, etc.	
l'adresse (fem.)	*address*
mon adresse, ton adresse, etc.	
la maison	*house*
ma maison, ta maison, etc.	

3. Look at the English side and go through the cards saying the French equivalent of the noun preceded by the correct form of the possessive adjective, again concentrating on the singular forms.

Flashcard

1. For review, create one card for each of the persons (1st, 2nd, and 3rd singular and plural) with an example of the different forms, including an example of a feminine singular noun beginning with a vowel.

mon livre, ma chaise, mes devoirs	*my (book, chair, homework)*
mon idée (fem.)	*my (idea)*
ton livre, ta chaise, tes devoirs,	*your*
votre (livre, chaise), vos (livres, chaises)	*your*

2. On the card for the 3rd person singular, to reinforce the fact that *his* *her* and *its* can be either **son** or **sa**, write French sentences with 3rd pers. sing. possessive adjectives modifying masculine and feminine singular nouns.

Il prend son livre.	*He takes his (her) book.*
Elle prend son livre.	*She takes his (her) book.*
Il prend sa chaise.	*He takes his (her) chair.*
Elle prend sa chaise.	*She takes his (her) chair.*

WHAT IS AN INTERROGATIVE ADJECTIVE?

An **INTERROGATIVE ADJECTIVE** is a word that asks for information about a noun.

> *Which* book do you want?
>
> asks information about the noun *book*

IN ENGLISH

The words ***which*** and ***what*** are interrogative adjectives when they come in front of a noun and are used to ask a question about that noun.

> *Which* teacher is teaching the course?
> *What* courses are you taking?

IN FRENCH

There is only one interrogative adjective, **quel**. It changes to agree in gender and number with the noun it modifies. Therefore, in order to say *"which* book" or *"what* dress," start by analyzing the noun *book* or *dress.*

- noun modified is masculine singular → **quel**
  > ***What*** *book is on the table?*
  > **Livre** *(book)* is masculine singular,
  >   so the word for *what* must be masculine singular.
  > **Quel** livre est sur la table?

- noun modified is masculine plural → **quels**
  > ***What*** *books are on the table?*
  > **Livres** *(books)* is masculine plural,
  >   so the word for *what* must be masculine plural.
  > **Quels** livres sont sur la table?

- noun modified is feminine singular → **quelle**
  > ***Which*** *dress do you want?*
  > **Robe** *(dress)* is feminine singular,
  >   so the word for *which* must be feminine singular.
  > **Quelle** robe voulez-vous?

- noun modified is feminine plural → **quelles**
  > ***Which*** *dresses do you want?*
  > **Robes** *(dresses)* is feminine plural,
  >   so the word for *which* must be feminine plural.
  > **Quelles** robes voulez-vous?

1

10

20

30

In the sentences above, the noun that the interrogative adjective modifies is easy to identify because the noun and the adjective are next to one another. However, the noun modified is harder to identify when it is separated from the interrogative adjective. As you can see in the examples below, restructuring the sentences will help you identify the noun with which the interrogative adjective must agree.

>**What** *is your address?*
>>Restructure: *"What address is yours?"*
>
>**Quelle** est votre adresse?
>>fem. sing.

>**Which** *are his favorite books?*
>>Restructure: *"Which books are his favorites?"*
>
>**Quels** sont ses livres préférés?
>>masc. pl.

CAREFUL — The word *what* is not always an interrogative adjective. In the sentence *"What* is on the table?" it is an interrogative pronoun (see *What is an Interrogative Pronoun?*, p. 139). It is important that you distinguish one from the other because, in French, different words are used and they follow different rules.

WHAT IS A DEMONSTRATIVE ADJECTIVE?

A **DEMONSTRATIVE ADJECTIVE** is a word used to point out a noun or to point to a noun.

> *This* book is interesting.
> |
> points out the noun *book*

IN ENGLISH

The demonstrative adjectives are **this** and **that** in the singular and **these** and **those** in the plural. They are rare examples of English adjectives agreeing in number with the noun they modify: *this* changes to *these* and *that* changes to *those* when they modify a plural noun.

SINGULAR	PLURAL
this cat	*these* cats
that man	*those* men

This and *these* refer to a person or object near the speaker, and *that* and *those* refer to a person or object away from the speaker.

IN FRENCH

There is only one demonstrative adjective, **ce**. As all French adjectives it changes to agree in gender and number with the noun it modifies. Therefore, in order to say *"that* book" or *"this* dress," start by analyzing the noun *book* or *dress*.

- noun modified is masculine singular and starts with a consonant → **ce**

> Ce livre est sur la table.
> > **Livre** *(book)* is masculine singular,
> > so the word for *this* must be masculine singular.
> ***This*** *(or **that**) book is on the table.*

- noun modified is masculine singular and starts with a vowel → **cet**

> Cet appartement est grand.
> > **Appartement** *(apartment)* is masculine singular.
> > Since it begins with a vowel, the word for *this* must be **cet**.
> ***This*** *(or **that**) apartment is large.*

- noun modified is feminine singular → **cette**

  Cette robe est jolie.
  > **Robe** *(dress)* is feminine singular,
  > so the word for *this* must be feminine singular.

  *This (or **that**) dress is pretty.*

- noun modified is plural → **ces**

  Ces livres sont sur la table.
  > **Livres** *(books)* is plural,
  > so the word for *these* must be plural.

  *These (or **those**) books are on the table.*

To distinguish between what is close to the speaker *(this, these)* from what is far from the speaker *(that, those)* **-ci** or **-là** can be added after the noun: **-ci** indicates that the noun is close to the speaker, **-là** that the noun is far from the speaker.

> **Ces** livres-**ci** sont chers; **ces** livres-**là** ne sont pas chers.
> *These books **(here)** are expensive; **those** books **(there)** are not expensive.*

WHAT IS AN ADVERB?

An **ADVERB** is a word that describes a verb, an adjective, or
another adverb. It indicates manner, degree, time, place.[1]

> Mary drives *well*.
> | |
>   verb adverb

> The house is *very* big.
> | |
>   adverb adjective

> The girl ran *too quickly*.
> | |
>   adverb adverb

IN ENGLISH

There are different types of adverbs:

- an **ADVERB OF MANNER** answers the question *how?* Adverbs
  of manner are the most common and they are easy to
  recognize because they end with *-ly*.

  > Mary sings *beautifully*.
  > *Beautifully* describes the verb *sings*; it tells you how Mary sings.

- an **ADVERB OF DEGREE** answers the question *how much?*
  > Paul does *well* in class.

- an **ADVERB OF TIME** answers the question *when?*
  > He will come *soon*.

- an **ADVERB OF PLACE** answers the question *where?*
  > The old were left *behind*.

IN FRENCH

Most adverbs of manner can be recognized by the ending
-ment that corresponds to the English ending *-ly*.

joli**ment**	*beautifully*
générale**ment**	*generally*
heureuse**ment**	*happily*

You will have to memorize adverbs as vocabulary items.
The most important fact for you to remember is that
adverbs are invariable; i.e., they never change form.

[1]In English and in French, the structure for comparing adverbs is the same as the structure for comparing adjectives (see *What is Meant by Comparison of Adjectives?*, p. 89).

CAREFUL — While adverbs in English are usually placed after the subject of the sentence, in French they are usually placed after the verb:

> *I **always** study at home.*
> |
>   verb

> J'étudie **toujours** à la maison.
> |
>   verb

Consult your textbook for the placement of adverbs.

ADVERB OR ADJECTIVE?

Because adverbs are invariable and French adjectives must agree with the noun they modify, it is important that you distinguish one from the other. When you write a sentence in French, always make sure that adjectives agree with the noun or pronoun they modify and that adverbs remain unchanged.

> *The **tall** girl walked **slowly**.*
>> *Tall* modifies the noun *girl*; it is an adjective. *Slowly* modifies the verb *walked* (it describes how the girl walked); it is an adverb.
>
> La **grande** fille marchait **lentement**.
> |_____| |
>   fem. sing.   adverb

> *The **tall** boy walked **slowly**.*
>> *Tall* modifies the noun *boy*; it is an adjective. *Slowly* modifies the verb *walked* (it describes how the boy walked); it is an adverb.
>
> Le **grand** garçon marchait **lentement**.
> |_____| |
>   masc. sing.   adverb

CAREFUL — In colloquial English adjectives are often used instead of adverbs. In French, however, the usage of an adjective for an adverb is incorrect; you must use an adverb.

> *He speaks **real slow**.* ➞ *He speaks **really slowly**.*
> | | | |
>   adj. adj.   adverb adverb
>   **vrai lent**   modifies modifies
>   verb   adverb
>   *speaks really*

> Il parle **vraiment lentement**.
> | |
>   adverb   adverb

To distinguish between an adjective and an adverb identify the part of speech of the word modified: if the word in question modifies a noun it is an adjective, if it modifies a verb, an adjective, or an adverb it is an adverb.

The student writes *good* English.
> *Good* modifies the noun *English;* it is an adjective.

The student writes *well.*   [80]
> *Well* modifies the verb *writes;* it is an adverb.

*The **good** students speak French **well.***

adjective	adverb
modifies	modifies
noun *student*	verb *speak*

Les **bons** étudiants parlent **bien** le français.

adjective (masc. pl.)	adverb

STUDY TIPS — ADVERBS

Flashcards (see *Tips for Learning Vocabulary*, p. 1)

1. Create flashcards for each French adverb you learn and its English equivalent.

    souvent   *often*

2. When you learn the placement of adverbs in a sentence, add sample sentences illustrating their placement. (Refer to your textbook for the placement of adverbs.)

    | Elle parle souvent de son frère. | *She often speaks of her brother.* |
    | Elle a souvent parlé de son frère. | *She often spoke of her brother.* |

CHAPTER

34

WHAT IS A CONJUNCTION?

A **CONJUNCTION** is a word that links two or more words or groups of words.

He had to choose between good *and* evil.

conjunction

They left *because* they were bored.

conjunction

IN ENGLISH

There are two kinds of conjunctions: coordinating and subordinating.

- a **COORDINATING CONJUNCTION** joins words, **PHRASES**, i.e., a group of words without a verb, or **CLAUSES**, i.e., a group of words with a verb, to one another. The major coordinating conjunctions are *and, but, or, nor, for,* and *yet.*

good *or* evil

word   word

over the river *and* through the woods

phrase   phrase

They invited us, *but* we couldn't go.

clause   clause

In the last example, each of the two clauses, "they invited us" and "we couldn't go," expresses a complete thought; each clause is, therefore, a complete sentence that could stand alone. When a clause expresses a complete thought it is called a **MAIN CLAUSE**. Above, the coordinating conjunction *but* links two main clauses.

- a **SUBORDINATING CONJUNCTION** joins a main clause to a dependent clause; it *subordinates* one clause to another. A **DEPENDENT CLAUSE** does not express a complete thought; it is, therefore, not a complete sentence and cannot stand alone. There are various types of dependent clauses. A clause introduced by a subordinating conjunction is called a **SUBORDINATE CLAUSE**. Typical subordinating conjunctions are *before, after, since, although, because, if, unless, so that, while, that,* and *when.*

subordinate clause   main clause

Although we were invited, we didn't go.

subordinating
conjunction

They left *because* they were bored.

subordinating
conjunction

He said *(that)* he was tired.

subordinating
conjunction

    In the above examples, "although we were invited," "because they were bored" and "(that) he was tired" are subordinate clauses. They are not complete sentences and each is introduced by a subordinating conjunction.

    Notice that the subordinating conjunction *that* is in parentheses because it is often omitted in English.

IN FRENCH

Conjunctions must be memorized as vocabulary items. Just as adverbs and prepositions, conjunctions are invariable (i.e., they never change their form). Be sure to memorize the conjunctions that are followed by the subjunctive mood instead of the indicative (see *What is the Subjunctive?*, p. 83).

    STUDY TIPS — CONJUNCTIONS AND THE SUBJUNCTIVE

Flashcards (see *Tips for Learning Vocabulary*, p. 1)
1. Create flashcards indicating French conjunctions and their English equivalent.

       parce que   *because*

2. When you learn the subjunctive, indicate the conjunctions that are followed by the subjunctive instead of the indicative. Add an example as reinforcement.

       bien que (+ subj.)   *although*
       Il est sorti   *He went out*
       bien qu'il soit malade.   *although he is sick.*

Practice
Write a series of sentences using the various conjunctions. Make sure to put the following verb in the subjunctive, if the conjunction requires it.

CHAPTER

35

WHAT IS A PREPOSITION?

A **PREPOSITION** is a word with a meaning often related to time or space that links nouns to nouns, nouns to verbs and different parts of a sentence to one another.

prepositional phrase
Paul has an appointment *after* school.
preposition   object of preposition

The noun or pronoun following the preposition is called the **OBJECT OF THE PREPOSITION**. The preposition plus its object is called a **PREPOSITIONAL PHRASE**.

IN ENGLISH

Prepositions normally indicate location, direction, or time.

- prepositions showing location or direction

    Paul was *in* the car.
    Mary put the books *on* the table.
    The students came directly *from* class.
    Mary went *to* school.

- prepositions showing time and date

    French people go on vacation *in* August.
    On Mondays, they go to the university.
    I'm meeting him *at* 4:30 today.
    We're studying *before* taking the exam.
    Most people work *from* nine to five.

Other frequently used prepositions are: *during, since, with, between, of, about.*

IN FRENCH

You will have to memorize prepositions as vocabulary, paying special attention to their meaning and use. Prepositions are invariable; that is, they never change form (they never become plural, nor do they have gender).

CAREFUL — Prepositions are tricky. Every language uses prepositions differently. Do not assume that the same preposition is used in French as in English, or even that a preposition will be needed in French when one is needed in English and vice versa.

ENGLISH	FRENCH

CHANGE OF PREPOSITION

| to be angry *with* | être fâché **contre** *(against)* |
| to be *on* the plane | être **dans** *(in)* l'avion |

40

PREPOSITION	NO PREPOSITION
to wait *for*	attendre
to look *at*	regarder

NO PREPOSITION	PREPOSITION
to telephone	téléphoner **à**
to answer	répondre **à**

A dictionary will usually give you the verb and the preposition that follows it, when one is required. Do not translate an English verb + preposition with a word-for-word French equivalent (see p. 26).

50

STUDY TIPS — PREPOSITIONS

Flashcards (see *Tips for Learning Vocabulary*, p. 1)
Be careful when creating flashcards for prepositions: one English preposition can have several French equivalents and vice versa. Always learn a preposition in a short sentence illustrating its usage.

1. Prepositions indicating the position of one object or person in relation to another are the easiest to learn because there is usually only one French equivalent.

sur	*on top of*
Le livre est sur la table.	*The book is on the table.*
derrière	*behind, in back of*
Jean est derrière Marie.	*John is behind Mary.*

2. Prepositions such as *to, at, in* + place and *by, on, in* + a means of transportation have many French equivalents because they vary according to the noun that follows. Rather than creating separate cards for these prepositions, indicate them on the appropriate noun cards.

la ville	*town*
Je vais en ville.	*I'm going to town.*
la bibliothèque	*library*
Je vais à la bibliothèque.	*I'm going to the library.*
l'avion (masc.)	*plane*
Je vais en avion.	*I'm going by plane.*
la bicyclette	*bike*
Je vais à bicyclette.	*I'm going by bike.*

3. When you learn a verb that is usually followed by a preposition + noun, indicate the preposition on the verb card and write a short sentence to illustrate its use.

répondre (à)   *to answer*
Je réponds à sa lettre.   *I'm answering his letter.*

4. When you learn a verb that requires a preposition when it is followed by an infinitive, indicate the preposition on the verb card and write a short sentence to illustrate its use.

décider de + infinitive   *to decide*
J'ai décidé de partir.   *I decided to leave.*

Practice

1. Following the examples under 1 above, think of two objects (or persons) and write French sentences using prepositions placing the objects (or persons) in various positions in relation to one another.

2. Following the examples under 2 above, sort out the noun cards indicating a place or a means of transportation and create short sentences using them with the appropriate preposition.

WHAT ARE OBJECTS?

OBJECTS are nouns or pronouns indicating towards what or whom the action of the verb is directed.

> Paul writes a *letter*.
> | | |
> verb object

> He speaks to *Mary*.
> | | |
> verb object

> The boy left with *his father*.
> | | |
> verb object

Verbs can be classified as to whether or not they can take an object.

- a **TRANSITIVE VERB** (*v.t.* in the dictionary) is a verb that can have an object.

  > The boy *threw* the ball.
  > |
  > transitive

- an **INTRANSITIVE VERB** (*v.i.* in the dictionary) is a verb that never has an object.

  > Paul *is sleeping*.
  > |
  > intransitive

We will study the three types of objects separately: direct object, indirect object, and object of a preposition. Since noun and pronoun objects are identified by using the same set of questions, we have limited the examples in this section to noun objects (see *What is a Noun?*, p. 8). For examples with pronoun objects see *What is an Object Pronoun?*, p. 115 and *What is a Disjunctive Pronoun?*, p. 123.

DIRECT OBJECT
IN ENGLISH

A direct object is a noun or pronoun that receives the action of the verb directly, without a preposition between the verb and the noun or pronoun object. It answers the question *whom?* or *what?* asked after the verb.[1]

---

[1]In this section, we will consider active sentences only (see *What is Meant by Active and Passive Voice?*, p. 165).

Paul sees *Mary*.
> Paul sees whom? Mary.
> *Mary* is the direct object.

Paul writes *a letter*.
> Paul writes what? A letter.
> *A letter* is the direct object.

IN FRENCH

As in English, a direct object is a noun or pronoun that receives the action of the verb directly, without a preposition.

*Paul sees **Mary**.*
Paul voit **Marie**.
> No preposition separates **Marie** from the verb **voit**. Therefore, **Marie** is a direct object.

*Paul writes **a letter**.*
Paul écrit **une lettre**.
> No preposition separates **une lettre** from the verb **écrit**. Therefore, **une lettre** is a direct object.

As with English verbs, French verbs can be transitive or intransitive depending on whether or not they are followed by a direct object.

INDIRECT OBJECT
IN ENGLISH

An indirect object is a noun or pronoun that receives the action of the verb indirectly, with the preposition *to* relating it to the verb. It answers the question *to whom?* or *to what?* asked after the verb.

She spoke *to her friends*.
> She spoke to whom? Her friends.
> *Her friends* is the indirect object.

He gave the painting *to the museum*.
> He gave a painting to what? The museum.
> *The museum* is the indirect object.

IN FRENCH

As in English, an indirect object is a noun or pronoun that receives the action of the verb indirectly, with the preposition à *(to)* relating it to the verb.

Elle a parlé **à ses amis**.
*She spoke **to her friends**.*

Il a donné le tableau **au musée**.
> à + le = au

*He gave the painting **to the museum**.*

Nouns that are indirect objects are easy to identify in French because they are always preceded by the preposition **à**.

SENTENCES WITH A DIRECT AND AN INDIRECT OBJECT

A sentence may contain both a direct object and an indirect object that can be either nouns or pronouns. In this section we shall speak only of nouns as objects because pronoun objects follow a different word order.

IN ENGLISH

When a sentence has both a direct and an indirect object, the following two word orders are possible:

1. subject (S) + verb (V) + indirect object (IO) + direct object (DO)

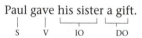

     Paul gave his sister a gift.
      S   V   IO   DO

Who gave a gift? Paul.
Paul is the subject.

Paul gave *what?* A gift.
A gift is the direct object.

Paul gave a gift *to whom?* His sister.
His sister is the indirect object.

2. subject + verb + direct object + *to* + indirect object

     Paul gave a gift to his sister.
      S   V DO   IO

The first structure, under 1, is the most common. However, because there is no "to" preceding the indirect object, it is more difficult to identify its function than in the second structure.

Regardless of the word order, the function of the words in these two sentences is the same because they answer the same question. Be sure to ask the questions to establish the function of words in a sentence.

IN FRENCH

Unlike English, there is only one word order possible (structure 2) when a sentence has both a direct and an indirect object: subject + verb + direct object + **à** + indirect object.

Paul a donné **un cadeau à sa soeur**.

S   V   DO   IO

*Paul gave **his sister a gift**.*
*Paul gave **a gift to his sister**.*

OBJECT OF A PREPOSITION

IN ENGLISH

An object of a preposition is a noun or pronoun that receives the action of the verb through a preposition other than *to*. (Objects of the preposition *to* are considered indirect objects and are discussed above.) It answers the question *whom?* or *what?* asked after the preposition.

> Paul works *for Mary*.
>> Paul works *for whom?* Mary.
>> *Mary* is the object of the preposition *for*.

> The baby eats *with a spoon*.
>> The baby eats *with what?* A spoon.
>> *A spoon* is the object of the preposition *with*.

IN FRENCH

As in English, an object of a preposition is a noun or pronoun that receives the action of the verb through a preposition other than **à** *(to)*.

> Paul travaille **pour Marie**.
> *Paul works **for Mary**.*

> Le bébé mange **avec une cuillère**.
> *The baby eats **with a spoon**.*

RELATIONSHIP OF A VERB TO ITS OBJECT

The relationship between a verb and its object is often different in English and French. For example, a verb may take a direct object in English and an indirect object in French, or an object of a preposition in English and a direct object in French. Therefore, when you learn a French verb it is important to find out if it is followed by a preposition and if so which one. Your textbook, as well as dictionaries, will indicate when a French verb needs a preposition before an object (see p. 26).

Here are differences you are likely to encounter.

1. ENGLISH: object of a preposition → FRENCH: direct object

I am looking for the book.

Function in English: object of a preposition   160
I am looking *for what*? The book.
The book is the object of the preposition *for*.

Je cherche **le livre**.

to look for → **chercher**
Function in French: direct object

Many common verbs require an indirect object or an object of a preposition in English, but a direct object in French.

*to listen **to***	écouter
*to look **at***	regarder
*to wait **for***	attendre

170

2. ENGLISH: direct object → FRENCH: indirect object

She phones her friends every day.

Function in English: direct object
She phones *whom*? Her friends.
Her friends is the direct object.

Elle téléphone **à ses amis** tous les jours.

to telephone → **téléphoner à**
Function in French: indirect object

A few common verbs require a direct object in English   180
and an indirect object in French.

to obey	obéir **à**
to resemble	ressembler **à**
to ask (a person)	demander **à** (une personne)

3. ENGLISH: direct object → FRENCH: object of a preposition

The student enters the classroom.

Function in English: direct object
The student enters *what*? The classroom.
The classroom is the direct object.

L'étudiant entre dans **la salle de classe**.   190

to enter → **entrer dans**
Function in French: object of the preposition **dans**

Your ability to recognize the three types of objects is essential. With pronouns, for instance, a different French pronoun is used for the English pronoun *him* depending on whether *him* is a direct object (**le**) or an indirect object (**lui**). (See *What is an Object Pronoun?*, p. 115).

SUMMARY

200 The different types of objects in a sentence can be identified by establishing whether they answer a question that requires a preposition or not and, if so, which one.

DIRECT OBJECT — An object that receives the action of the verb directly, without a preposition.

INDIRECT OBJECT — An object that receives the action of the verb indirectly, through the preposition *to*.

OBJECT OF A PREPOSITION — An object that receives the action of the verb through a preposition other than *to*.

210 **CAREFUL** — Always identify the function of a word within the language in which you are working; do not use English patterns in French.

WHAT IS AN OBJECT PRONOUN?

An **OBJECT PRONOUN** is a pronoun replacing a noun as direct or   1
indirect object of a verb (see pp. 109-11 in *What are Objects?*).

> Paul saw *her*.
>> Paul saw whom? Answer: Her.
>> *Her* is the object of the verb *saw*.

Pronouns change according to their function in a sentence.
Pronouns used as subjects are studied in *What is a Subject Pronoun?*, p. 32. Other types of pronouns are studied in *What is a Disjunctive Pronoun?*, p. 123.

IN ENGLISH   10

Most object pronouns are different from subject pronouns;
however, the same form is used for a direct and indirect
objects.

		SUBJECT	**OBJECT**
SINGULAR			
1ST PERSON		I	**me**
2ND PERSON		you	**you**
3RD PERSON	{	he	**him**
		she	**her**
		it	**it**
PLURAL			
1ST PERSON		we	**us**
2ND PERSON		you	**you**
3RD PERSON		they	**them**

Let us look at two examples.

> She saw *me*.
>> direct object → object pronoun

> He lent the car to *me*.
>> indirect object → object pronoun

IN FRENCH

As in English, the pronouns used as objects are different
from the ones used as subjects. Unlike English, however,
the form of the object pronoun often changes depending
whether it is a direct or an indirect object.

FRENCH DIRECT OBJECT PRONOUNS

First make sure that the French verb takes a direct object. Remember that English and French verbs don't always take the same type of objects and that when working in French you have to establish the type of object required by the French verb (see pp. 112-3).

Since the pattern of 1ˢᵗ and 2ⁿᵈ person direct object pronouns is different from the pattern of 3ʳᵈ person direct object pronouns, we have divided the French direct object pronouns into these two categories:

1ˢᵗ and 2ⁿᵈ person sing. and pl. (me, you, us)

1ˢᵗ and 2ⁿᵈ persons direct object pronouns have only one form per person. Just select the form you need from the chart below.

	SUBJECT	DIRECT OBJECT	SUBJECT	DIRECT OBJECT
SINGULAR 1ˢᵗ PERSON 2ⁿᵈ PERSON	je tu	me te	*I* *you*	*me* *you*
PLURAL 1ˢᵗ PERSON 2ⁿᵈ PERSON	nous vous	nous vous	*we* *you*	*us* *you*

To simplify our examples we have used the verb **to see** *(voir)* because both the English and the French verbs take a direct object.

> *Paul sees **me**.*
>   1. Identify the verb: to see
>   2. What is the French equivalent: **voir**
>   3. Does the French verb need a preposition before an object: No
>   4. Function of pronoun in French: direct object
>   5. Selection: **me**
> Paul **me** voit.
>
> *Paul sees **you**.*
> Paul **te** voit.
> Paul **vous** voit.
>
> *Paul sees **us**.*
> Paul **nous** voit.

Establishing the function of **nous** and **vous** can be confusing. Not only are the same forms used as subject and object, but both subject and object pronouns are placed before the verb. In case of doubt, look at the verb.

Remember that verbs agree with their subject. If **nous** is the   80
subject, the verb will end in **-ons**; if it doesn't, **nous** is an
object of some kind. The same is true with **vous.** If it is the
subject of the verb, the ending of regular verbs will be **-ez.**

> Vous **nous** voyez tous les jours.
>> **Nous** cannot be the subject because the verb **voir** doesn't
>> end in **-ons**. The subject of **voyez** can only be **vous.** There-
>> fore, **nous** must be an object pronoun.
>
> *You see **us** every day.*

3ʳᵈ person sing. and pl. (him, her, it, them)

3ʳᵈ person singular direct object pronouns have a masculine   90
and feminine form. The gender of *it* depends on the gender
of its antecedent; that is, the noun that it is replacing.

	SUBJECT	**DIRECT OBJECT**	**SUBJECT**	**DIRECT OBJECT**
SINGULAR				
MASCULINE	il	le	*he, it*	*him, it*
FEMININE	elle	la	*she, it*	*her, it*
PLURAL				
MASCULINE	ils	les	*they*	*them*
FEMININE	elles			

For our examples we have again used the verb **to see**
(voir) because both the English and the French verbs take a
direct object.

> *Do you see Paul? Yes, I see **him.***
> Voyez-vous Paul? Oui, je **le** vois.
>
> *Do you see Mary? Yes, I see **her.***
> Voyez-vous Marie? Oui, je **la** vois.
>
> *Do you see the girls? Yes, I see **them.***   110
> Voyez-vous les jeunes filles? Oui, je **les** vois.

It as a direct object requires that you establish the gender
of its antecedent.

> *Do you see the book? Yes, I see **it.***
> Voyez-vous le livre? Oui, je **le** vois.
>> 1. Antecedent: **Livre** *(book)* is masculine.
>> 2. Gender of *it:* masculine → **le**
>
> *Do you see the table? Yes, I see **it.***
> Voyez-vous la table? Oui, je **la** vois.   120
>> 1. Antecedent: **Table** *(table)* is feminine.
>> 2. Gender of *it:* feminine → **la**

FRENCH INDIRECT OBJECT PRONOUNS

First, make sure that the French verb takes an indirect object. Remember that English and French verbs don't always take the same type of objects and that when working in French you have to establish the type of object required by the French verb (see pp. 112-3).

Unlike noun indirect objects that are always preceded by the preposition à in French (see p. 111), pronoun indirect objects are not preceded by à. The form of the pronoun itself indicates that it is indirect.

Since the pattern of 1st and 2nd person indirect object pronouns is different from the pattern of 3rd person indirect object pronouns, we have divided the French indirect object pronouns into these two categories.

1st and 2nd persons sing. and pl. (me, you, us)

1st and 2nd person indirect object pronouns are the same as the direct object pronouns. Just select the form you need from the chart below.

	SUBJECT	INDIRECT OBJECT	SUBJECT	INDIRECT OBJECT
SINGULAR 1ST PERSON 2ND PERSON	je tu	**me** **te**	*I* *you*	*(to) me* *(to) you*
PLURAL 1ST PERSON 2ND PERSON	nous vous	**nous** **vous**	*we* *you*	*(to) us* *(to) you*

To simplify our examples, we have chosen the verb *to speak to* (**parler à**) that takes an indirect object both in English and in French.

> *Paul speaks **to me**.*
> > 1. Identify the verb: to speak
> > 2. What is the French equivalent: **parler**
> > 3. Is the French verb followed by à: Yes
> > 4. Function of the pronoun in French: indirect object
> Paul **me** parle.
> |
>   indirect object pronoun

> *Paul speaks **to you**.*
> Paul **te** parle.
> Paul **vous** parle.

> *Paul speaks **to us**.*
> Paul **nous** parle.

130

140

150

160

3rd person sing. and pl. (him, her, them)

There are two types of 3rd person indirect object pronouns.

1. 3rd person indirect object pronouns referring to people and animals have a singular and plural form.

170

	DIRECT OBJECT	INDIRECT OBJECT	DIRECT OBJECT	INDIRECT OBJECT
SINGULAR MASCULINE FEMININE	le la	lui	*him, it* *her, it*	*(to) him* *(to) her*
PLURAL MASCULINE FEMININE	les	leur	*them*	*(to) them*

Are you speaking to Mary? Yes, I am speaking to her.
1. Identify the verb: to speak
2. What is the French equivalent: **parler** 180
3. Does the French verb require the preposition à before an object? Yes
4. Function of the pronoun in French: indirect object
5. Number of antecedent: singular *(Mary)*
6. Selection: **lui**

Parlez-vous **à** Marie? Oui, je **lui** parle.

Are you speaking to Paul and Mary? Yes, I am speaking to them.
1 - 4. See above.
5. Number of antecedent: plural *(Paul and Mary)*
6. Selection: **leur**

Parlez-vous **à** Paul et à Marie? Oui, je **leur** parle. 190

2. 3rd person indirect object pronouns referring to things and ideas have only one form → **y**

Are you answering the letter? Yes, I am answering it.
1. Identify the verb: to answer
2. What is the French equivalent: **répondre**
3. Does the French verb require the preposition à before an object? Yes
4. Function of the pronoun in French: indirect object
5. Type of antecedent: thing *(the letter)*
6. Selection: **y** 200

Répondez-vous **à** la lettre? Oui, j'**y** réponds.

CAREFUL — In English, object pronouns are always placed after the verb. In French, however, they are usually placed before the verb. Consult your textbook for the placement of pronouns when a verb has both a direct and an indirect object pronoun.

SUMMARY OF OBJECT PRONOUNS

Below is a chart of the French equivalent of English object pronouns.

DO → Direct object in the French sentence
IO   → Indirect object in the French sentence

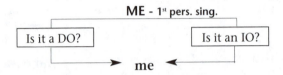

ME - 1st pers. sing.

| Is it a DO? | | Is it an IO? |

me

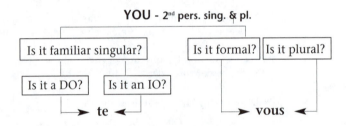

YOU - 2nd pers. sing. & pl.

Is it familiar singular?   Is it formal? Is it plural?

Is it a DO?   Is it an IO?

te   vous

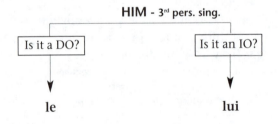

HIM - 3rd pers. sing.

Is it a DO?   Is it an IO?

le   lui

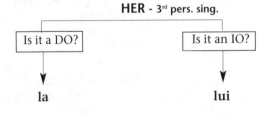

HER - 3rd pers. sing.

Is it a DO?   Is it an IO?

la   lui

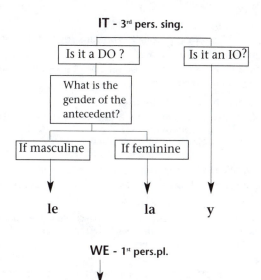

IT - 3ʳᵈ pers. sing.

Is it a DO ? Is it an IO?

What is the gender of the antecedent?

If masculine If feminine

le **la** **y**

WE - 1ˢᵗ pers.pl.

nous

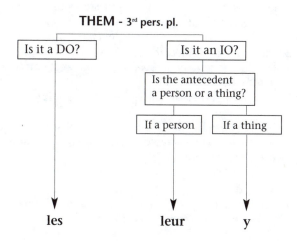

THEM - 3ʳᵈ pers. pl.

Is it a DO? Is it an IO?

Is the antecedent a person or a thing?

If a person If a thing

les **leur** **y**

Pattern (see *Tips For Learning Word Forms,* p. 3)
Learn the various types of object pronouns separately (direct, indirect and disjunctive, see also Chapter 38).

1. Look for similarities between direct object pronouns and other parts of speech. Refer to the charts on pp. 116-9.

   What similarities can you think of?
   - 1st & 2nd pers. sing.: initial m- and t- same as the initial letters of the possessive adjectives (mon, ton)
   - 1st & 2nd pers. pl.: same as subject pronouns
   - 3rd pers. sing. & pl.: same as definite articles

2. When you learn indirect object pronouns, look for similarities with direct object pronouns as well as other parts of speech.

   What similarities do you notice?
   - 1st, 2nd pers. sing. & pl.: same forms for direct and indirect object pronouns
   - 3rd pers. pl.: indirect object pronoun is the same as the singular form of the 3rd pers. pl. possessive adjective (leur).

Practice

1. Since function determines a pronoun's form it is important to learn object pronouns in a sentence.

2. Write a series of short French sentences with masculine, feminine and plural direct objects. Rewrite the sentences replacing the direct object with the appropriate object pronoun.

Il donne le cadeau.	*He gives the gift.*
Il le donne.	*He gives it.*

3. Add an indirect object to the original sentences you created under 2. Rewrite the sentences replacing the indirect object with the appropriate object pronoun.

Il donne le cadeau à sa soeur.	*He gives his sister the gift.*
Il lui donne le cadeau.	*He gives her the gift.*

4. Replace both the direct and indirect objects with pronouns in the sentences you've created under 3. (Refer to your textbook for the correct word order.)

Il le lui donne.	*He gives it to her.*

Flashcard

1. On the subject pronoun flashcards, add sentences illustrating the pronoun's direct and indirect forms.

il	*he, it*
Je la (le) vois.	*I see her (him, it).*
Je lui donne un livre.	*I give her (him) a book.*
Le livre est pour lui (elle).	*The book is for him (her).*

2. Review by going through the cards on the English side and creating French sentences illustrating the various forms.

WHAT IS A DISJUNCTIVE PRONOUN?

A DISJUNCTIVE PRONOUN (also known as STRESSED or TONIC PRONOUN) is used as a one-word answer to a question and as an object of a preposition. [1]

> Who's doing the cooking? *Me.*
> Paul arrived after *me.*

Pronouns change according to their function in a sentence. Pronouns used as subjects are studied in *What is a Subject Pronoun?*, p. 32. Other types of pronouns are studied in *What is an Object Pronoun?*, p. 115.

IN ENGLISH [10]

English disjunctive pronouns have the same form as object pronouns (see p. 115).

	OBJECT/DISJUNCTIVE PRONOUNS
SINGULAR	
1ST PERSON	me
2ND PERSON	you
3RD PERSON	{ him her
PLURAL	
1ST PERSON	us
2ND PERSON	you
3RD PERSON	them

[20]

Disjunctive pronouns are used primarily in two instances:

1. in short answers when the identity of the person referred to is obvious from the context

> Who are you looking at? *Him.*
> Whom did he stay with? *Us.*

2. when the pronoun is an object of a preposition (see p. 112)

> I'm staying *with **him**.* [30]
> |
>   preposition
> He arrived *before **us**.*
> |
>   preposition

IN FRENCH

Disjunctive pronouns, LES PRONOMS PERSONNELS TONIQUES in French, have a different form from direct and indirect object pronouns (see charts pp.120-1).

	DISJUNCTIVE PRONOUNS	
SINGULAR		
1ˢᵀ PERSON	moi	*me*
2ᴺᴰ PERSON	toi	*you*
3ᴿᴰ PERSON	{ lui { elle	*him* *her*
PLURAL		
1ˢᵀ PERSON	nous	*us*
2ᴺᴰ PERSON	vous	*you*
3ᴿᴰ PERSON	{ eux { elles	*them* *them*

Disjunctive pronouns are used in the following instances.

1. As in English, disjunctive pronouns are used in short answers when the identity of the person referred to is obvious from the context.

> *Who is there?* **Me.**
> Qui est là? **Moi.**

> *Whom do you want to see?* **Him.**
> Qui voulez-vous voir? **Lui.**
>   masc. sing.

> *Whom do you want to see?* **Her.**
> Qui voulez-vous voir? **Elle.**
>   fem. sing.

2. In French, a disjunctive pronoun is often used before a subject pronoun for emphasis or to contrast one subject with another.

> *What language do you speak?*
> *I speak French, she speaks English.*
> Quelle langue parlez-vous?
> **Moi, je** parle français, **elle, elle** parle anglais.
>
> disjunctive +   disjunctive +
> subject   subject
> pronouns   pronouns

See the section below for the usage of the disjunctive forms when a pronoun is an object of a preposition.

FRENCH PRONOUNS AS OBJECTS OF A PREPOSITION

Remember that English and French don't always use the same prepositions and that when working in French you have to establish the preposition used in French.

If the pronoun follows the preposition **à** it is an indirect object and takes an indirect object pronoun, not a disjunctive (see pp. 118-9 in *What is an Object Pronoun?*).

80

Let us look at the French pronouns used as objects of a preposition to see how they are selected. Because the pattern of pronouns the 1ˢᵗ and 2ⁿᵈ persons is different from the pattern of the pronouns of the 3ʳᵈ person, we have divided French pronouns objects of a preposition into these two categories.

1ˢᵗ and 2ⁿᵈ person singular and plural (me, you, us)

1ˢᵗ and 2ⁿᵈ person pronouns objects of a preposition are the disjunctive forms and are placed after the preposition.

90

	SUBJECT		OBJECT OF A PREPOSITION	
SINGULAR				
1ˢᵗ PERSON	je	*I*	prép. + **moi**	*prep. + me*
2ⁿᵈ PERSON	tu	*you*	prép. + **toi**	*prep. + you*
PLURAL				
1ˢᵗ PERSON	nous	*we*	prép. + **nous**	*prep. + us*
2ⁿᵈ PERSON	vous	*you*	prép. + **vous**	*prep. + you*

Here are a few examples.

*Is the book **for** Paul ? No, it's **for me.***
*No, it's **for you.***
*No, it's **for us.***

100

   1. Identify the verb: to be
   2. What is the French equivalent: **être**
   3. Is the French verb followed by a preposition? Yes.
   4. What preposition? **pour** *(for)*
   5. Function of pronoun in French: object of preposition
   6. Selection: **moi, toi (vous), nous**

Est-ce que le livre est **pour** Paul? Non, il est **pour moi.**
Non, il est **pour toi (vous).**
Non, il est **pour nous.**

3ʳᵈ person singular and plural (him, her, it, them)

110

There are two types of object of preposition pronouns:

1. 3ʳᵈ person pronouns objects of a preposition referring to people and animals have a masculine and feminine form in the singular and plural.

	SUBJECT		OBJECT OF PREPOSITION	
SINGULAR				
MASCULINE	il	*he*	prép. + **lui**	*prep. + him*
FEMININE	elle	*she*	prép. + **elle**	*prep. + her*
PLURAL				
MASCULINE	ils	*they*	prép. + **eux**	*prep. + them*
FEMININE	elles	*they*	prép. + **elles**	*prep. + them*

120

Is the book for Paul ? Yes, it is for him.
1. Identify the verb: to be
2. What is the French equivalent: **être**
3. Is the French verb followed by a preposition? Yes
4. What preposition? **pour** *(for)*
5. Function of pronoun in French: object of preposition
6. Gender of antecedent: masculine *(Paul)*
7. Selection: **lui**

₁₃₀ Est-ce que le livre est **pour** Paul? Oui, il est **pour lui.**

Is the book for Mary? Yes, it is for her.
1 - 5. See above.
6. Gender of antecedent: feminine *(Mary)*
7. Selection: **elle**
Est-ce que le livre est **pour** Marie? Oui, il est **pour elle.**

Is the book for the boys? Yes it is for them.
1 - 5. See above.
6. Gender of antecedent: masculine *(boys)*
₁₄₀ 7. Selection: **eux**
Est-ce que le livre est **pour** les garçons? Oui, il est **pour eux.**

Is the book for the girls? Yes it is for them.
1 - 5. See above.
6. Gender of antecedent: feminine *(girls)*
7. Selection: **elles**
Est-ce que le livre est **pour** les filles? Oui, il est **pour elles.**

2. 3rd person pronouns that refer to things or ideas that are objects of the preposition **de** *(of)* use the pronoun **en**
₁₅₀ which stands for both the **de** and the pronoun.

Here are some examples:
I liked the book so I am going to talk about it.
1. Identify the verb: to talk (to talk *about* → parler **de**)
2. What is the French equivalent: **parler**
3. Is the French verb followed by **de**: Yes
4. Function of pronoun in French: object of preposition **de**
5. Type of antecedent: thing *(book)*
6. Selection: **en** (replaces **de** + pronoun)
J'ai aimé le livre alors je vais **en** parler.

₁₆₀ *I liked these books so I am going to talk about them.*
1 - 6. See above.
J'ai aimé ces livres alors je vais **en** parler.

Consult your textbook for other uses of disjunctive pronouns and the pronoun **en.**

SUMMARY OF OBJECT AND DISJUNCTIVE PRONOUNS

Below is a flow chart of the steps you have to follow to find the French equivalent of each English disjunctive and object pronoun. It is important that the steps be done in sequence, because each step depends on the previous one.

DO → Direct object in the French sentence
IO → Indirect object in the French sentence
DP → Disjunctive pronoun or object of preposition in the French sentence

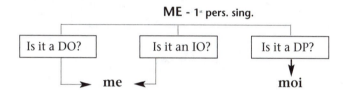

ME - 1ˢᵗ pers. sing.

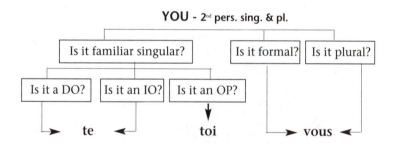

YOU - 2ⁿᵈ pers. sing. & pl.

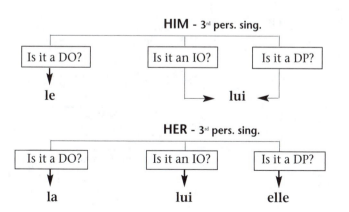

HIM - 3ʳᵈ pers. sing.

HER - 3ʳᵈ pers. sing.

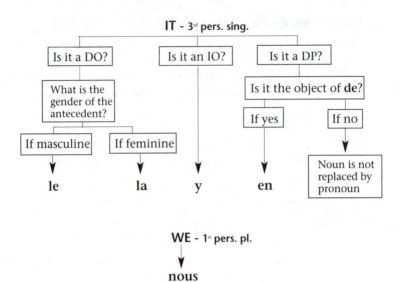

IT - 3ʳᵈ pers. sing.

| Is it a DO? | Is it an IO? | Is it a DP? |

What is the gender of the antecedent?

Is it the object of **de**?

| If yes | If no |

| If masculine | If feminine |

le   **la**   **y**   **en**   Noun is not replaced by pronoun

WE - 1ˢᵗ pers. pl.

nous

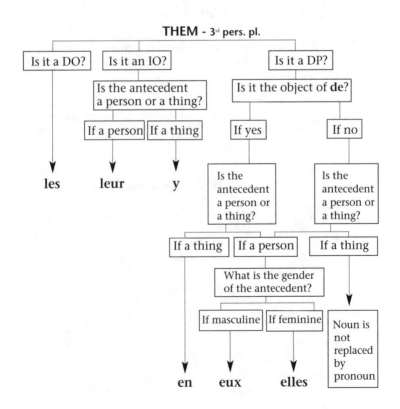

THEM - 3ʳᵈ pers. pl.

| Is it a DO? | Is it an IO? | Is it a DP? |

Is the antecedent a person or a thing?

Is it the object of **de**?

| If a person | If a thing |

| If yes | If no |

les   **leur**   **y**

Is the antecedent a person or a thing?

Is the antecedent a person or a thing?

| If a thing | If a person | | If a thing |

What is the gender of the antecedent?

| If masculine | If feminine |

en   **eux**   **elles**   Noun is not replaced by pronoun

WHAT ARE REFLEXIVE PRONOUNS AND VERBS?

A **REFLEXIVE VERB** is a verb that is accompanied by a pronoun, called a **REFLEXIVE PRONOUN**, that serves *to reflect* the action of the verb back to the subject.

subject = reflexive pronoun → the same person

She *cut herself* with the knife.

reflexive verb

IN ENGLISH

Many regular verbs can take on a reflexive meaning by adding a reflexive pronoun.

The child *dresses* the doll.

regular verb

The child *dresses herself.*

verb + reflexive pronoun

Reflexive pronouns end with *-self* in the singular and *-selves* in the plural.

		SUBJECT PRONOUN + VERB +		REFLEXIVE PRONOUN
SINGULAR				
1ST PERSON		I	wash	myself
2ND PERSON		you	wash	yourself
3RD PERSON	{	he	washes	himself
		she	washes	herself
		it	washes	itself
PLURAL				
1ST PERSON		we	wash	ourselves
2ND PERSON		you	wash	yourselves
3RD PERSON		they	wash	themselves

As the subject changes so does the reflexive pronoun, because they both refer to the same person or object.

I cut myself.
Paul and Mary blamed *themselves* for the accident.

Although the subject pronoun *you* is the same for the singular and plural, there is a difference in the reflexive pronouns: *yourself* is used when you are speaking to one person (singular) and *yourselves* is used when you are speaking to more than one (plural).

> Paul, did you make *yourself* a sandwich?
> Children, make sure you wash *yourselves* properly.

Reflexive verbs can be in any tense: *I wash myself, I washed myself, I will wash myself,* etc.

IN FRENCH

As in English, reflexive verbs, LES VERBES PRONOMINAUX in French, are formed with a verb and a reflexive pronoun.

Here are the French reflexive pronouns:

SINGULAR			
1ST PERSON	me	*myself*	
2ND PERSON	te	*yourself*	
3RD PERSON	se	*himself, herself, itself, oneself*	
PLURAL			
1ST PERSON	nous	*ourselves*	
2ND PERSON	vous	*yourself, yourselves*	
3RD PERSON	se	*themselves*	

In the dictionary, reflexive verbs are listed under the regular verb. For instance, under **laver** *(to wash)* you will also find **se laver** *(to wash oneself)*.

Look at the conjugation of **se laver**. Notice two things: 1. as in English, the reflexive pronoun changes according to the person of the conjugation, and 2. unlike English, the reflexive pronoun is placed before the verb.

	SUBJECT PRONOUN +	REFLEXIVE PRONOUN +	VERB
SINGULAR			
1ST PERSON	je	me	lave
2ND PERSON	tu	te	laves
3RD PERSON	il / elle / on	se	lave
PLURAL			
1ST PERSON	nous	nous	lavons
2ND PERSON	vous	vous	lavez
3RD PERSON	ils / elles	se	lavent

Reflexive verbs can be conjugated in all tenses. The subject and reflexive pronouns remain the same, regardless of the tense of the verb: **je me** *laverai* (**futur**); **je me** *suis lavé* (**passé composé**).

The compound tenses of reflexive verbs are always con- 80
jugated with the auxiliary **être** *(to be)*; however, the rules
of agreement of the past participle of reflexive verbs are
different from the rules of agreement of the past participle
of regular verbs (see pp. 62-3). Be sure to consult your
French textbook for these rules of agreement.

Reflexive verbs are common in French. There are many
expressions that are not reflexive in English, but whose
French equivalent is a reflexive verb. You will have to
memorize these idiomatic expressions.

to get up	se lever *(to get oneself up)* 90
to go to bed	se coucher *(to put oneself to bed)*
to wake up	se réveiller *(to wake oneself up)*
to be bored	s'ennuyer *(to bore oneself)*
to have a good time	s'amuser *(to amuse oneself)*
to make a mistake	se tromper *(to mistake oneself)*
to stop	s'arrêter *(to stop oneself)*
to take a walk	se promener *(to walk oneself)*

In all the examples above, the French reflexive pronouns
have a meaning equivalent to the English reflexive pronouns listed on p. 129 *(myself, yourself, himself,* etc.). This 100
is not always the case. French reflexive pronouns can also
indicate reciprocal action (see below).

CAREFUL — In compound tenses reflexive verbs are conjugated with the auxiliary **être**, but they are conjugated with
the auxiliary **avoir** when they are regular non-reflexive
verbs.

REGULAR VERB	REFLEXIVE VERB
Il **a coupé** le pain.	Il **s'est coupé** en se rasant.
*He **cut** the bread.*	*He **cut himself** shaving.*
Jean **a acheté** un livre.	Jean **s'est acheté** un livre. 110
*John **bought** a book.*	*John **bought himself** a book.*
Marie **a fait** le dîner.	Marie **s'est fait** une robe.
*Mary **made** dinner.*	*Mary **made herself** a dress.*

RECIPROCAL ACTION
IN ENGLISH

English uses a regular verb followed by the expression
"each other" to express reciprocal action, that is, an action
between two or more persons or things.

The dog and the cat looked at *each other*.

> The expression "each other" tells us that the action of 120
> *looking* was reciprocal, i.e., the dog looked at the cat and the
> cat looked at the dog.

Our children call *each other* every day.
> The expression "each other" tells us that the action of
> *calling* is reciprocal, i.e., the various children call one
> another every day.

Since reciprocal verbs require that more than one person
or thing be involved, the verb is always plural.

IN FRENCH

French uses reflexive pronouns to express an action that is
reciprocal.

Le chien et le chat **se** regardaient.
*The dog and the cat looked at **each other**.*

Nos enfants **se** téléphonent tous les jours.
*Our children call **each other** every day.*

Context will often indicate to you if the meaning of the
French pronoun is reflexive or reciprocal.

Les danseurs **se** regardent dans le miroir.
> The information "dans le miroir" leads us to believe that
> they are looking at themselves. Therefore, **se** is reflexive.
*The dancers look at **themselves** in the mirror.*
                                         |
                                    reflexive

However, if no extra information is given, the meaning
of the French sentence is ambiguous.

Les danseurs **se regardent**.
*The dancers **look at themselves**.* → REFLEXIVE
*The dancers **look at each other**.* → RECIPROCAL

One way to avoid ambiguity, and to indicate that the
meaning is reciprocal rather than reflexive, is to add an
expression equivalent to "each other," such as "**l'un
l'autre**" (singular) or "**les uns les autres**" (plural).

Le chien et le chat **se** regardent **l'un l'autre**.
   | | |_____|
 sing.   sing.   sing.
*The dog and the cat look at **each other**.*

Les danseurs **se** regardent **les uns les autres**.
                | |_____|
             plural   plural
*The dancers look at **each other**.*

Consult your textbook for detailed explanations.

WHAT IS A POSSESSIVE PRONOUN?

A **POSSESSIVE PRONOUN** is a word that replaces a noun and indicates the possessor of that noun. The word *possessive* comes from *possess,* to own.

> Whose house is that? It's *mine.*
>> *Mine* replaces the noun *house,* the object possessed, and shows who possesses it, "me."

IN ENGLISH

Here is a list of the possessive pronouns:

SINGULAR POSSESSOR

1ST PERSON		mine
2ND PERSON		yours
	MASCULINE	his
3RD PERSON	FEMININE	hers
	NEUTER	its ·

PLURAL POSSESSOR

1ST PERSON	ours
2ND PERSON	yours
3RD PERSON	theirs

Possessive pronouns only refer to the possessor, not to the object possessed.

> My car is red; what color is John's? *His* is blue.
>> 3rd pers. masc. sing.

> John's car is blue. What color is yours? *Mine* is white.
>> 1st pers. sing.

>> Although the object possessed is the same *(car),* different possessive pronouns *(his* and *mine)* are used because the possessors are different *(John* and *me).*

> Is that John's house? Yes, it is *his.*
> Are those John's keys? Yes, they are *his.*
>> Although the objects possessed are different *(house* and *keys),* the same possessive pronoun *(his)* is used because the possessor is the same *(John).*

IN FRENCH

Like English, a French possessive pronoun refers to the possessor. Unlike English, it also agrees, like all French pronouns, in gender and number with its **ANTECEDENT,** that is with the person or object possessed. Also, the possessive pronoun is preceded by a definite article that also agrees in gender and number with the antecedent.

Let us analyze an English sentence in order to find the correct form of the French possessive pronoun.

> *Where are your books?* ***Mine** are in the living room.*
>
> 1. Find the possessor: *Mine* → 1st person singular
> 2. Find antecedent: *Mine* refers to *books*
> 3. Establish the gender and number of the French equivalent of the antecedent: *books*
> 4. Choose the ending of the possessive pronoun that corresponds in gender and number to step 3 above.
> 5. Choose the definite article that corresponds in gender and number to step 3 above.
>
> Où sont tes livres? **Les miens** sont dans le salon.
>
> 1. 1st person singular possessor *mine* → first letter of the possessive pronoun → **m-**
> 2. Antecedent: *books* → **livres**
> 3. **Livres** → masculine plural
> 4. Masculine plural ending → **-iens** (see p. 135)
> 5. Masculine plural definite article → **les**

Let us look at the French possessive pronouns to see how they are formed. Because the pattern of possessive pronouns for a singular possessor is different from the pattern of possessive pronouns for a plural possessor, we have divided the French possessive pronouns into these two groups.

SINGULAR POSSESSOR (1ST, 2ND AND 3RD PERS. SING.)
mine, yours (tu-form), his/hers

Each of these possessive pronouns has four forms depending on the gender and number of the antecedent. To choose the proper form follow these steps.

1. Indicate the possessor. This will be shown by the first letter of the possessive pronoun. (They are the same initial letters as the possessive adjectives, see *What is a Possessive Adjective?*, p. 92.)

mine	**m-**
yours (**tu**-form)	**t-**
his *hers*	**s-**

2. Establish the gender and number of the antecedent and choose the definite article and the ending that corresponds to its gender and number.

- noun possessed is masculine singular → **le** + first letter of the possessor + **-ien**

A qui est ce **livre?**	C'est **le mien.**
|	C'est **le tien.**
masculine singular	C'est **le sien.**
*Whose **book** is that?*	*It is **mine.***
	*It is **yours.***
	*It is **his (hers).***

- noun possessed is feminine singular → **la** + first letter of the possessor + **-ienne**

A qui est cette **lettre?**	C'est **la mienne.**
|	C'est **la tienne.**
feminine singular	C'est **la sienne.**
*Whose **letter** is that?*	*It is **mine.***
	*It is **yours.***
	*It is **his (hers).***

- noun possessed is masculine plural → **les** + first letter of the possessor + **-iens**

A qui sont ces **livres?**	Ce sont **les miens.**
|	Ce sont **les tiens.**
masculine plural	Ce sont **les siens.**
*Whose **books** are those?*	*They are **mine.***
	*They are **yours.***
	*They are **his (hers).***

- noun possessed is feminine plural → **les** + first letter of the possessor + **-iennes**

A qui sont ces **lettres?**	Ce sont **les miennes.**
|	Ce sont **les tiennes.**
feminine plural	Ce sont **les siennes.**
*Whose **letters** are those?*	*They are **mine.***
	*They are **yours.***
	*They are **his (hers).***

3. Select the proper form according to the two steps above.

Let us apply these steps to some examples.

*Mary is looking at her photos. John is looking at **yours.***
1. Possessor: *yours* [familiar] → 2nd pers. sing. → **t-**
2. Noun possessed: **Photos** *(photos)* is feminine plural → **les**
3. Selection: **les** + **t-** + **-iennes**

Marie regarde ses photos. Jean regarde **les tiennes.**

*Lend me your book. No, I'll lend you **hers.***
    1. Possessor: *hers* → 3rd pers. sing. → **s-**
    2. Noun possessed: **Livre** *(book)* is masculine singular → **le**
    3. Selection: **le + s- + -ien**
Prêtez-moi votre livre. Non, je vous prêterai **le sien.**

PLURAL POSSESSOR (1ST, 2ND AND 3RD PERS. PL.)
ours, yours (vous-form), theirs

In French, each of these possessive pronouns has one form that is preceded by the definite article corresponding to the gender and number of the antecedent. To choose the proper form, follow these steps:

1. Indicate the possessor.

ours	**nôtre**
yours	**vôtre**
theirs	**leur**

2. Establish the gender and number of the antecedent and choose the definite article that corresponds to its gender and number.
- noun possessed is masculine singular → **le**
- noun possessed is feminine singular → **la**
- noun possessed is plural → **les** + add an "**s**" to the possessive pronoun

3. Select the proper form according to the two steps above.

Let us apply these steps to some examples.

*I took my letter. Did you take **yours?***
    1. Possessor: *yours* [formal]→ 2nd pers. pl. → **vôtre**
    2. Noun possessed: **Lettre** *(letter)* is feminine singular → **la**
    3. Selection: **la vôtre**
J'ai pris ma lettre. Avez-vous pris **la vôtre**?

*I do not have my books, but Paul and Mary have **theirs.***
    1. Possessor: *theirs* → 3rd pers. pl. → **leur**
    2. Noun possessed: **Livres** *(books)* is plural → **les**
    3. Selection: **les leur- + - s**
Je n'ai pas mes livres, mais Paul et Marie ont **les leurs.**

Although **vôtre** is classified as "second person plural," it can refer to just one person when used as a formal form of address (see p. 33).

SUMMARY

Here is a chart you can use as a reference.

Possessor Singular		Noun possessed	
		Singular	Plural
mine	MASC.	le mien	les miens
	FEM.	la mienne	les miennes
yours (**tu**-form)	MASC.	le tien	les tiens
	FEM.	la tienne	les tiennes
his, hers	MASC.	le sien	les siens
	FEM.	la sienne	les siennes
Possessor Plural		Noun possessed	
		Singular	Plural
ours	MASC.	le nôtre	les nôtres
	FEM.	la nôtre	
yours (**vous**- form)	MASC.	le vôtre	les vôtres
	FEM.	la vôtre	
theirs	MASC.	le leur	les leurs
	FEM.	la leur	

170

180

STUDY TIPS — POSSESSIVE PRONOUNS

Pattern (see *Tips For Learning Word Forms*, p. 3)
1. It will be easy for you to establish a pattern if you follow our instructions above under "Singular Possessor" and "Plural Possessor" (pp. 134-6).
2. Note the circumflex over **nôtre** and **vôtre** which, along with the definite article, distinguishes these possessive pronouns from the possessive adjectives **notre** and **votre**.

Practice
1. You can use the same selection of noun flashcards you used to practice possessive adjectives (see p. 96).
2. Look at the French side and go through the cards replacing the nouns with the correct form of the possessive pronoun. Concentrate on the singular forms **le mien, le tien, le sien** since they are the forms that change.

un jardin	*garden*
le mien, le tien, etc.	*mine*
une maison	*house*
la mienne, la tienne, etc.	*mine*

3. Write short questions in French requiring an answer with a possessive pronoun.

C'est ton livre?	*Is that your book?*
Oui, c'est le mien.	*Yes, it is mine.*
Ce sont tes clés?	*Are those your keys?*
Oui, ce sont les miennes.	*Yes, they are mine.*

4. Give negative answers to the questions you wrote under 3 above so that the answer will require a different possessive pronoun from the one given above.

C'est ton livre?	*Is that your book?*
Non, c'est le sien.	*No, it is hers (his).*
Ce sont tes clés?	*Are those your keys?*
Non, ce sont les leurs.	*No, they are theirs.*

Flashcard

1. For review, create one card per person (1ˢᵗ, 2ⁿᵈ, and 3ʳᵈ person singular and plural) with an example of the different forms.

   le mien, la mienne, les miens, les miennes   *mine*

2. On the cards for the 3ʳᵈ person singular and plural, to reinforce the fact that *his* or *hers* can be either **le sien, la sienne, les siens, les siennes**, write French questions requiring answers equivalent to *his* and *hers*.

C'est le livre de Marie (Paul)?	*Is it Mary's (Paul's) book?*
Oui, c'est le sien.	*Yes, it's hers (his).*
Ce sont les livres de Marie (Paul)?	*Are they Mary's (Paul's) books?*
Oui, ce sont les siens.	*Yes, they're hers (his).*
C'est la clé de Marie (Paul)?	*Is it Mary's (Paul's) key?*
Oui, c'est la sienne.	*Yes, it's hers (his).*

CHAPTER

41

WHAT IS AN INTERROGATIVE PRONOUN?

An **INTERROGATIVE PRONOUN** is a word that replaces a noun and introduces a question. The word *interrogative* comes from *interrogate,* to question.

> *Who* is coming for dinner?
>
> replaces a person

> *What* did you eat for dinner?
>
> replaces a thing

In both English and French, a different interrogative pronoun is used depending on whether it refers to a "person" (human beings and live animals) or a "thing" (objects and ideas). Also, the form of the interrogative pronoun often changes according to its function in the sentence: subject, direct object, indirect object, and object of a preposition. We shall look at each function separately.

SUBJECT

(see *What is a Subject?*, p. 28)

IN ENGLISH

A different interrogative pronoun is used depending on whether it refers to a person or a thing.

PERSON — *Who* is used for the subject of the sentence.

> *Who* speaks French?
>
> subject verb 3ʳᵈ pers. sing.

THING — *What* is used for the subject of the sentence.

> *What* is on the table?
>
> subject

An interrogative pronoun used as subject is always followed directly by the verb in the 3ʳᵈ person singular.

IN FRENCH

As in English, a different interrogative pronoun is used depending on whether it refers to a person or a thing.

PERSON — **Qui** + verb *or* **Qui est-ce qui** + verb

> **Qui** parle français?
> **Qui est-ce qui** parle français?
>
> verb 3ʳᵈ pers. sing.
> *Who speaks French?*

THING — **Qu'est-ce qui** + verb

Qu'est-ce qui est sur la table?
What is on the table?

As in English, an interrogative pronoun used as subject is always followed directly by a verb in the 3rd person singular.

DIRECT OBJECT

(see pp. 109-10 in *What are Objects?*)

IN ENGLISH

A different interrogative pronoun is used depending on whether it refers to a person or a thing.

PERSON — ***Whom*** is used for the object of the sentence.

Whom do you know here?
    | |
direct object subject

Because *whom* is often replaced by *who* (ex: *"Who* do you know here?"), the form of the interrogative pronoun will not tell you if it is a subject or a direct object. It is only by analyzing the sentence that you will learn the function of the interrogative pronoun.

THING — ***What*** is used for the object of the sentence.

What do you want?
  |
direct object

IN FRENCH

Regardless of the function of the French interrogative pronoun, the forms with **est-ce que** take the normal word order, subject + verb, whereas the other forms are followed by an inversion, namely, verb + subject (see *What are Declarative and Interrogative Sentences?*, p. 50).

As in English, a different interrogative pronoun is used depending on whether it refers to a person or a thing.

PERSON — **Qui est-ce que** + subject + verb *or* **Qui** + verb + subject

Qui est-ce que vous connaissez?
              | |
            subject + verb

Qui connaissez-vous?
    | |
   verb + subject

Who(m) do you know?

Thing — **Qu'est-ce que** + subject + verb *or* **Que** + verb + subject

> **Qu'est-ce que** vous voulez?
>   subject + verb

> **Que** voulez-vous?
>   verb + subject
>
> *What do you want?*

INDIRECT OBJECT AND OBJECT OF A PREPOSITION

(see pp. 110-1, p. 112 in *What are Objects?*)

IN ENGLISH

It is difficult to identify an English interrogative pronoun functioning as an indirect object or as an object of a preposition because the interrogative pronoun is often separated from the preposition of which it is the object. When a preposition is separated from its object and placed at the end of a sentence or question it is called a DANGLING PREPOSITION.

> *Who* did you speak *to?*
> interr. pronoun preposition

> *Who* did you get the book *from?*
> interr. pronoun   preposition

To enable you to establish if an interrogative pronoun is an indirect object or an object of a preposition, you will have to change the structure of the sentence so that the preposition is placed before the interrogative pronoun. This restructuring will not only make it easier for you to identify the function of the pronoun, but it will also establish the word order for the French sentence.

The following sentences have been restructured to avoid a dangling preposition.

> *Who* are you giving the book *to?* →
> interr. pronoun   preposition
> *To whom* are you giving the book?
> indirect object

> *What* are you contributing *to?* →
> interr. pronoun   preposition
> *To what* are you contributing?
> indirect object

Who are you going out *with?* →
With whom are you going out?

object of the preposition *with*

What are you writing *with?* →
With what are you writing?

object of the preposition *with*

The same form of the interrogative pronoun is used as an indirect object and as an object of a preposition. However, a different interrogative pronoun is used depending on whether it refers to a person or a thing.

PERSON — *Who (whom)* is used for indirect objects and objects of a preposition.

Who did you speak *to?* →
To whom did you speak?

indirect object

Who did you get the book *from?* →
From whom did you get the book?

object of preposition *from*

THING — *What* is used for indirect objects and objects of a preposition.

What did you pay *with?* →
With what did you pay?

object of preposition *with*

IN FRENCH

As in English, the same form of the interrogative pronoun is used as an indirect object (always preceded by the preposition **à***)* and as an object of a preposition (always preceded by a preposition other than **à***)*. As in English, a different interrogative pronoun is used depending on whether it refers to a person or a thing.

PERSON — Preposition + **qui est-ce que** + subject + verb *or* Preposition + **qui** + verb + subject

A qui est-ce que vous donnez le livre?

subject + verb

A qui donnez-vous le livre?

verb + subject

To whom are you giving the book?

indirect object

Avec qui est-ce que vous sortez?
| |
subject + verb

Avec qui sortez-vous?
| |
verb + subject

With whom are you going out?
|
object of preposition *with*

THING — Preposition + **quoi est-ce que** + subject + verb *or*
Preposition + **quoi** + verb + subject

A quoi est-ce que vous contribuez?
| |
subject + verb

A quoi contribuez-vous?
| |
verb + subject

To what are you contributing?
|
indirect object

Avec quoi est-ce que vous écrivez?
| |
subject + verb

Avec quoi écrivez-vous?
| |
verb + subject

With what are you writing?
|
object of the preposition *with*

CAREFUL — Once again we remind you that some French verbs take direct objects, while the equivalent English verbs take an indirect object and vice-versa (see pp. 112-3). Make sure that you determine the function of the pronoun in French.

SUMMARY

To choose the correct form of French interrogative pronouns, proceed with the following three steps:

1. Determine the function of the interrogative pronoun in the French sentence (subject, direct object, indirect object or object of a preposition).
2. Establish whether the pronoun refers to a person or a thing.
3. Refer to the chart on the next page.

	SUBJECT	**DIRECT OBJECT**	**INDIRECT OBJECT AND OBJECT OF A PREPOSITION**
PERSON	*who* qui est-ce qui qui	*who(m)* qui est-ce que qui (+ inversion)	*preposition + who(m)* prép. + qui est-ce que prép. + qui (+ inversion)
THING	*what* qu'est-ce qui	*what* qu'est-ce que que (+ inversion)	*preposition + what* prép. + quoi est-ce-que prép. + quoi (+ inversion)

"WHICH (ONE), WHICH (ONES)"

There is another interrogative pronoun that we will examine because it does not follow the same pattern as the ones above.

IN ENGLISH

Which (one), which (ones) are used in questions that request the selection of one *(which one,* singular) or more than one *(which ones,* plural) from a group that has already been mentioned. The words *one* and *ones* are often omitted. These interrogative pronouns can refer to both persons and things and do not change according to function; they may be used subjects, direct objects, indirect objects, and objects of a preposition.

All the teachers are here. *Which one* teaches French?
   group mentioned   singular subject

I have two cars. *Which one* do you want to take?
   group mentioned   singular direct object

The library has many books. *Which ones* do you want?
   group mentioned   plural direct object

He has a group of friends. *Which ones* does he live with?
   group mentioned   plural object of preposition *(with)*

IN FRENCH

As in English, these interrogative pronouns do not change according to function. Their form does change, however, according to gender and number. Their gender depends on the gender of their ANTECEDENT (i.e., the noun to which they refer), and their number depends on whether you want to say *which **one*** (singular) or *which **ones*** (plural).

		MASCULINE	FEMININE
which (one)	SINGULAR	lequel	laquelle
which (ones)	PLURAL	lesquels	lesquelles

250

To choose the proper form, follow these steps:
  1. Determine the antecedent of *which*.
  2. Determine the gender of the antecedent.
  3. Do you wish to say *which one* → singular or *which ones* → plural?
  4. Select the correct French form from the above chart.

Let us apply these steps to some examples.

260

All the books are here. **Which one** *is in French?*
    1. Antecedent: the books
    2. Gender: **Livres** *(books)* is masculine.
    3. Number: *One* is singular.
    4. Selection: masculine singular → **lequel**
Tous les livres sont ici. **Lequel** est en français?

I have two cars. **Which one** *do you want to take?*
    1. Antecedent: the cars
    2. Gender: **Voitures** *(cars)* is feminine.
    3. Number: *One* is singular.
    4. Selection: feminine singular → **laquelle**
J'ai deux voitures. **Laquelle** veux-tu prendre?

270

I have many books. **Which ones** *do you want to read?*
    1. Antecedent: books
    2. Gender: **Livres** *(books)* is masculine.
    3. Number: *Ones* is plural.
    4. Selection: masculine plural → **lesquels**
J'ai beaucoup de livres. **Lesquels** veux-tu lire?

Here are four girls; **which ones** *do you want to speak* **to?** →
Here are four girls; **to which ones** *do you want to speak?*
    1. Antecedent: girls
    2. Gender: **Filles** *(girls)* is feminine.
    3. Number: *Ones* is plural.
    4. Selection: feminine plural → à + lesquelles → **auxquelles**
Voici quatre filles; **auxquelles** voulez-vous parler?

280

There are two books. **Which one** *are you speaking* **about?** →
There are two books. **About which one** *are you speaking?*
    1. Antecedent: books
    2. Gender: **Livres** *(books)* is masculine.
    3. Number: *One* is singular.
    4. Selection: masculine singular → de + lequel → **duquel**
Il y a deux livres. **Duquel** parlez-vous?

290

Pattern (see *Tips for Learning Word Forms*, p. 3)
1. Look for a pattern that distinguishes the interrogative pronouns referring to people from those referring to things. Let's concentrate on interrogative pronouns using "est-ce que" or "est-ce qui." The distinction between people and things is found in the first word.

- PEOPLE — interrogative pronouns referring to people start with **qui** or preposition + **qui** (*Avec qui est-ce que tu étudies?*).
- THINGS — interrogative pronouns referring to things start with **qu'** or preposition + **quoi** (*Avec quoi est-ce que tu écris?*).

2. Look for a pattern that distinguishes interrogative pronouns functioning as subjects from those functioning as objects. The function is indicated by the ending, i.e., the words following "est-ce."
- SUBJECTS — interrogative pronoun subjects end in **qui**.
- OBJECTS — interrogative pronoun objects end in **que (qu')**.

3. If you wish to learn the inversion forms, refer to the chart on p. 144. Remember that after the beginning **qui, qu'** or preposition + **qui/quoi**, you invert the subject and verb so that you'll have verb + subject (*Avec qui études-tu?, Avec quoi écrivez-vous?*). EXCEPTION: If **qui** is the subject, it is followed by the verb (*Qui parle?*).

Practice
1. On a blank piece of paper write questions using the various French forms.
2. Write French sentences answering "who," "what" questions. Then write a series of questions in French and answer them.

SENTENCE: L'étudiante lave la voiture avec du savon.

QUESTION: Qui lave la voiture?
ANSWER: L'étudiante lave la voiture.

QUESTION: Qu'est-ce que l'étudiante lave?
ANSWER: Elle lave la voiture.

QUESTION: Avec quoi est-ce qu'elle lave la voiture?
ANSWER: Elle lave la voiture avec du savon.

Flashcard
For review, create a card with a short question illustrating each form.

WHAT IS A RELATIVE PRONOUN?

A **RELATIVE PRONOUN** is a word used at the beginning of a clause giving additional information about someone or something previously mentioned.

clause
additional information about *the book*

I'm reading the book *that* the teacher recommended.

A relative pronoun serves two purposes:

1. As a pronoun it stands for a noun previously mentioned. The noun to which it refers is called the **ANTECEDENT**.

   This is the boy *who* broke the window.

   antecedent of the relative pronoun *who*

2. It introduces a **SUBORDINATE CLAUSE**; that is, a group of words having a subject and a verb that cannot stand alone because it does not express a complete thought. A subordinate clause is dependent on a **MAIN CLAUSE**; that is, another group of words having a subject and a verb that can stand alone as a complete sentence.

   main clause   subordinate clause

   Here comes the boy *who broke the window.*

   verb   subject   subject   verb

A subordinate clause that starts with a relative pronoun is also called a **RELATIVE CLAUSE**. In the example above, the relative clause starts with the relative pronoun *who* and gives us additional information about the antecedent *boy*.

Relative clauses are very common. We use them in everyday speech without giving much thought as to how we construct them. Relative pronouns allow us to combine in a single sentence two thoughts that have a common element.

SENTENCE A   I met the teacher.
SENTENCE B   He teaches French.
COMBINED   I met the teacher *who* teaches French.

When sentences are combined with a relative pronoun, the relative pronoun can have different functions in the relative clause. It can be the subject, the direct object, the indirect object, or the object of a preposition. The relative pronoun used for each function often depends on whether its antecedent is a "person" (human beings and animals) or a "thing" (objects and ideas). Let's look at each function separately.

SUBJECT
(see *What is a Subject?*, p. 28)

IN ENGLISH

The relative pronoun used as subject depends on whether the antecedent is a person or a thing. The verb of the relative clause agrees with the antecedent of the relative pronoun.

PERSON — *Who* or *that* is used as subject of the relative clause.

> She is the student *who (that)* is learning French.
>
> antecedent   verb
> sing.   3rd pers. sing.

> They are the students *who (that)* are learning French.
>
> antecedent   verb
> pl.   3rd pers. pl.

THING — *Which* or *that* is used as subject of the relative clause.

> These are the books *that (which)* are so interesting.
>
> antecedent   verb
> pl.   3rd pers. pl.

Notice that the relative pronoun subject is always followed by a verb.

IN FRENCH

There is only one relative pronoun that can be used as subject of a relative clause, regardless of the antecedent, **qui**. As in English, the verb of the relative clause agrees with the antecedent of the relative pronoun.

> *This is the student **who** is learning French.*
> Voici l'étudiant **qui** apprend le français.
>
> antecedent   rel. pr.   verb
> sing.   3rd pers. sing.

*These are the books **which (that)** are so interesting.*
Voici les livres **qui** sont si intéressants.   80

        | | |

   antecedent   rel. pr.   verb
   pl.   3rd pers. pl.

As in English, the relative pronoun subject (**qui**) is always followed by a verb.

COMBINING SENTENCES: RELATIVE PRONOUN SUBJECT
IN ENGLISH
      SENTENCE A   The students passed the exam.
      SENTENCE B   They studied.

90

1. Identify the element the two sentences have in common.
    Both *the students* and *they* refer to the same persons.
2. The common element in the first sentence is called the **ANTECEDENT** of the relative pronoun; that is, the person or thing to which the relative pronoun refers. The relative pronoun always replaces the common element in the second sentence.
    The students is the antecedent.
    They will be replaced by a relative pronoun.

100

3. The relative pronoun in the relative clause has the same function as the word it replaces.
    They is the subject of *studied.* Therefore,
    the relative pronoun will be the subject of *studied.*
4. Choose the relative pronoun according to whether its antecedent is a person or a thing.
    They refers to *students.* Therefore, its antecedent is a person.
5. Select the relative pronoun.
    Who or *that* is the relative pronoun subject
    referring to a person.

110

6. Place the relative pronoun at the beginning of the second sentence, thus forming a relative clause.
    who studied
    that studied
7. Place the relative clause right after its antecedent.
    The students *who studied* passed the exam.
    The students *that studied* passed the exam.

      | |_____|

    antecedent   relative clause

IN FRENCH

SENTENCE A	Les étudiants ont réussi à l'examen.
SENTENCE B	Ils ont étudié.

Follow the steps under in English above, skipping step 4.

Les étudiants **qui** ont étudié ont réussi à l'examen.

      | |
  antecedent   relative clause

DIRECT OBJECT
(see pp. 109-10 in *What are Objects?*)

IN ENGLISH

The relative pronoun used as object depends on whether the antecedent is a person or a thing. The verb of the relative clause agrees with its subject. Since relative pronouns that function as objects of relative clauses are often omitted in English, we've put them between parentheses.

PERSON — ***Whom*** or ***that*** is used as direct object of a relative clause.

This is the student *(whom)* I saw yesterday.
This is the student *(that)* I saw yesterday.

          | |
  antecedent   direct object of *saw*

THING — ***Which*** or ***that*** is used as direct object of a relative clause.

This is the book *(which)* Paul bought.
This is the book *(that)* Paul bought.

      | |
  antecedent direct object of *bought*

Notice that the direct object relative pronoun, if expressed, is always followed by a subject (noun or pronoun) and its verb.

IN FRENCH

There is only one relative pronoun that can be used as direct object of a relative clause, **que** (**qu'** before a vowel). Unlike English, relative pronouns objects of relative clauses are never omitted (the equivalent English relative pronouns are between parentheses).

*This is the student **(whom)** he saw.*
Voici l'étudiant **qu'**il a vu.

*This is the book **(which)** I bought.*
Voici le livre **que** j'ai acheté.

As in English, the direct object relative pronoun (**que**) is always followed by a subject (noun or pronoun) and its verb.

COMBINING SENTENCES: RELATIVE PRONOUN DIRECT OBJECT

IN ENGLISH

SENTENCE A   The French teacher is nice.
SENTENCE B   I met him here.

1. Common element: *French teacher* and *him*
2. Element to be replaced: *him*
3. Function of *him*: direct object
4. Antecedent: *the French teacher* is a person.
5. Selection: *whom* or *that*
6. Relative clause: *whom (that)* I met here
7. Placement: antecedent (*the French teacher*) + relative clause

The French teacher (*whom*) I met here is nice.
The French teacher (*that*) I met here is nice.

    antecedent   relative clause

When the relative pronoun *whom* or *that* is left out ("The French teacher I met today is nice"), it is difficult to identify the two clauses.

IN FRENCH

SENTENCE A   Le professeur de français est gentil.
SENTENCE B   Je l'ai rencontré ici.

Follow the steps under in English above, skipping step 4.

Le professeur de français **que** j'ai rencontré ici est gentil.

   antecedent   relative clause

INDIRECT OBJECT AND OBJECT OF A PREPOSITION

(see pp. 110-1, p. 112 in *What are Objects?*)

A relative pronoun used as an indirect object is a relative pronoun object of the preposition *to*. A relative pronoun used as an object of a preposition is a relative pronoun object of a preposition other than *to* (see pp. 153-4).

Mary is the person *to whom* he gave the present.

    relative pronoun indirect object

Mary is the person *with whom* he went out.

    relative pronoun object of a preposition *(with)*

IN ENGLISH

It is difficult to identify the function of these relative pronouns in English because they are often separated from

170

180

190

200

the preposition of which they are the object. When a preposition is separated from its object and placed at the end of a sentence it is called a **DANGLING PREPOSITION** (see pp. 141-2).

Mary is the person *that* he went out *with*.

           relative pronoun   dangling preposition

The relative pronoun used as indirect object or as object of a preposition depends on whether the antecedent is a person or a thing. Since relative pronouns that function as indirect objects and as objects of a preposition are often omitted in English, we've put them between parentheses.

PERSON — ***Whom*** is used as indirect object and as object of a preposition.

Here is the student to *whom* I was speaking.

      antecedent   indirect object

Here is the student about *whom* I was speaking.

      antecedent   object of preposition *about*

The above sentences are usually expressed as follows:

Here is the student I was speaking *to*.
Here is the student I was speaking *about*.

These sentences without a relative pronoun and with a dangling preposition have to be restructured in order to establish the function of the relative pronoun that will have to be expressed in the French sentences. To restructure the English sentences, follow these steps:

1. Identify the antecedent.
2. Place the preposition after the antecedent.
3. Add the relative pronoun *whom* after the preposition.

SPOKEN ENGLISH	RESTRUCTURED
Here is the student I was speaking *to*.	Here is the student to *whom* I was speaking.
	indirect object of *was speaking*
Here is the student I was speaking *about*.	Here is the student *about whom* I was speaking.
	object of preposition *about*

THING — *Which* is used as indirect object and as object of a preposition.

Here is the museum he gave the painting *to*. 250
    | |
antecedent   dangling preposition

SPOKEN ENGLISH	RESTRUCTURED
Here is the museum	Here is the museum
he gave the painting *to*.	*to which* he gave the painting.
	indirect object of *gave*

IN FRENCH

Relative pronouns used as indirect objects or as objects of a preposition are divided into two main groups discussed 260 separately below: 1. objects of prepositions other than the preposition **de** (for ex., **à** *to*, **avec** *with*, etc.), and 2. objects of the preposition **de** *(of, etc.)*.

Unlike English, relative pronouns are never omitted in French. In the examples below, the equivalent English relative pronouns are between parentheses.

FRENCH RELATIVE PRONOUNS
OBJECTS OF PREPOSITIONS OTHER THAN "DE"

These relative pronouns are objects of all prepositions, i.e., **sans** *(without)*, **pour** *(for)*, etc., except the preposition **de**. 270 They include the relative pronouns used as indirect objects since they are objects of the preposition **à**. The form used depends on whether the antecedent is a person or a thing.

PERSON — Preposition + **qui**

*Here is the man (**that**) I am talking to.*
             |
       antecedent

SPOKEN ENGLISH	RESTRUCTURED
Here is the man	Here is the man
I am talking *to*.	*to whom* I am talking.

Voici l'homme **à qui** je parle.
                    |
           to talk to → **parler à**

THING — Preposition + **lequel**

Lequel must agree with the antecedent in gender and number. Also, following the preposition **à** the initial **le-** and **les-** become **au-** and **aux-**.

These are the pens (that) I write with.
|
antecedent

SPOKEN ENGLISH
These are the pens
I write *with*.

RESTRUCTURED
These are the pens
with which I write.

Voici les stylos **avec lesquels** j'écris.
| |
masc. pl.   masc. pl.

FRENCH RELATIVE PRONOUNS
OBJECTS OF THE PREPOSITION "DE"

When a relative pronoun is the object of the preposition **de** (*of,* etc.) there is one relative pronoun that is commonly used, **dont.** Unlike relative pronouns that follow other prepositions (see above), **dont** replaces the preposition **de** and its object.

Here is the man (that) I am talking about.
|
antecedent

SPOKEN ENGLISH
Here is the man
I am talking *about*.

RESTRUCTURED
Here is the man
about whom I am talking.

Voici l'homme **dont** je parle.
|
to talk about → **parler de**

We refer you to your French textbook for other ways to express relative pronouns that are objects of the preposition **de.**

COMBINING SENTENCES: RELATIVE PRONOUN OBJECT OF A PREPOSITION

IN ENGLISH

SENTENCE A   Mary read the book.
SENTENCE B   I was talking about it.

1. Common element: *the book* and *it*
2. Element to be replaced: *it*
3. Function of *it:* object of the preposition *about*
4. Antecedent: *The book* is a thing.
5. Selection: *which*
6. Relative clause: *about which* I was talking
7. Placement: antecedent *(book)* + relative clause

Mary read the book *about which* I was talking.
| |_____|
antecedent   relative clause

IN FRENCH

330

> SENTENCE A   Marie a lu le livre.
> SENTENCE B   Je parlais du livre.

Marie a lu le livre **dont** je parlais.

POSSESSIVE MODIFIER "WHOSE"

IN ENGLISH

The possessive modifier *whose* is a relative pronoun that does not change its form, regardless of its antecedent or function.

340

> This is the student *whose* mother came.
> Look at the house *whose* roof burned.

IN FRENCH

The French equivalent of the possessive modifier *whose* is **dont**.

> *This is the student **whose** mother came.*
> Voici l'étudiant **dont** la mère est venue.
>
> *Look at the house **whose** roof burned.*
> Regarde la maison **dont** le toît a brûlé.

350

SUMMARY

Here is a chart you can use as reference:

FUNCTION IN RELATIVE CLAUSE:	ANTECEDENT	
	PERSON	THING
SUBJECT	*who, that, which* **qui**	
DIRECT OBJECT	*whom, that, which* **que**	
OBJECT OF "DE"	*of (about, etc.) whom, which* **dont**	
OBJECT OF PREPOSITION (other than "de")	*preposition + whom* **prép. + qui**	*preposition + which* **prép. + lequel**, etc.
POSSESSIVE MODIFIER	*whose* **dont**	

360

To find the appropriate relative pronoun you must go through the following steps.

1. Find the relative clause.
   - restructure the English clause if there is a dangling preposition and
   - add the relative pronoun, if it has been omitted

370

2. Establish the function of the relative pronoun in the French sentence:

SUBJECT — If the relative pronoun is the subject of the English sentence, it will be the subject of the French sentence → **qui.**

DIRECT OBJECT — If the French verb takes a direct object → **que** or **qu'.**

OBJECT OF THE PREPOSITION "DE" — If the French verb is followed by the preposition **de** → **dont.**

380

OBJECT OF A PREPOSITION OTHER THAN "DE" — If the French verb is followed by a preposition other than **de:**
- if a person → preposition + **qui**
- if a thing → preposition + appropriate form of **lequel**

3. Select the relative pronoun (see chart p. 155).

4. Place the relative pronoun and its clause right after the antecedent.

Let us apply the steps outlined above to the following sentences:

390

*The plane **that** comes from Paris is late.*
1. Relative clause: that comes from Paris
2. Function of relative pronoun: subject of relative clause
3. Selection: **qui**
4. Antecedent: *plane* (**avion**)
5. Placement: antecedent (**avion**) + **qui** + clause

L'avion **qui** arrive de Paris est en retard.

*Here are the books **(that)** I bought yesterday.*
1. Relative clause: that I bought yesterday
2. Function of relative pronoun:

400

    direct object of **acheter** *(to buy)*
3. Selection: **que**
4. Antecedent: *books* (**livres**)
5. Placement: antecedent (**livres**) + **que** + clause

Voici les livres **que** j'ai achetés hier.

Notice the agreement of past participle **achetés** (masc. pl.) with the preceding direct object **que** referring to **livres** (masc. pl.), see p. 63.

*Where is the book **(that)** you need?*
1. Relative clause: that you need
2. Function of relative pronoun:

410

    object of preposition **de** *(to need → **avoir besoin de**)*
3. Selection: **dont**
4. Antecedent: *book* (**livre**)
5. Placement: antecedent (**livre**) + **dont** + clause

Où est le livre **dont** vous avez besoin?

Where is the table (which) he likes to work on?

SPOKEN ENGLISH	RESTRUCTURED
Where is the table	Where is the table *on which*
he likes to work *on?*	he likes to work?

    1. Relative clause: on which he likes to work

    2. Function of relative pronoun: object of preposition
       sur *(on)* + thing *(table)*

    3. Antecedent: *table* (**une table**) → fem. sing.

    4. Selection: **sur laquelle**

    5. Placement: antecedent (**table**) + **sur laquelle** + clause

Où est la table **sur laquelle** il aime travailler?

That is the boy (that) she is playing with.

SPOKEN ENGLISH	RESTRUCTURED
That is the boy	That is the boy
she is playing *with.*	*with whom* she is playing.

    1. Relative clause: with whom she is playing

    2. Function of relative pronoun: object of the preposition
       avec *(to play with → **jouer avec**)* + person *(boy)*

    3. Selection: **qui**

    4. Antecedent: *boy* (**garçon**)

    5. Placement: antecedent (**garçon**) + **avec qui** + clause

Voici le garçon **avec qui** elle joue.

Relative pronouns are tricky to handle and this handbook provides only a simple outline. Refer to your French textbook for additional rules.

RELATIVE PRONOUNS WITHOUT ANTECEDENTS

There are relative pronouns that do not refer to a specific noun or pronoun. Instead, they refer to an antecedent that has not been expressed or to an entire idea.

IN ENGLISH

There are two relative pronouns that can be used without an antecedent: ***what*** and ***which.***

What — does not refer to a specific noun or pronoun.

    I don't know *what* happened.
             |
          no antecedent
          subject

    Here is *what* I read.
        |
      no antecedent
      direct object

Which — refers to an entire idea, not to a specific noun or pronoun.

> She didn't do well, *which* is a pity.
>
>> antecedent: the fact that she didn't do well
>> subject of *is*

460

> You speak many languages, *which* I envy.
>
>> antecedent: the fact that you speak many languages
>> direct object of *envy (I* is the subject)

CAREFUL — The relative pronoun *what* (meaning "that which") should not be confused with other uses of *what*: as an interrogative pronoun, see p. 139 (**What** *do you want?* **Qu'est-ce que** vous voulez?) and as an interrogative adjective, see p. 97 (**What** *book do you want?* **Quel** livre voulez-vous?).

470

IN FRENCH

When a relative pronoun does not have a specific antecedent, the pronoun **ce** *(that)* is added to act as the antecedent. It is followed by the relative pronoun appropriate to its function in the relative clause, creating a structure that is word-for-word "that which."

Here are a few examples.

> *Here is* **what** *happened.*
>> 1. Relative clause: what happened
>> 2. No antecedent: add **ce**
>> 3. Function of relative pronoun: subject
>> 4. Selection: **ce qui**

480

Voici **ce qui** est arrivé.

> *Show me* **what** *you bought.*
>> 1. Relative clause: what you bought
>> 2. No antecedent: add **ce**
>> 3. Function of relative pronoun: direct object
>>   of **acheter** *(to buy)*
>> 4. Selection: **ce que**

490

Montrez-moi **ce que** vous avez acheté.

> *I don't know* **what** *he is talking about.*
>> 1. Relative clause: **what** he is talking *about* →
>>   Restructured: *about what* he is talking
>> 2. No antecedent: add **ce**
>> 3. Function of relative pronoun: object of preposition **de**
>>   *(to speak about* → **parler de**)
>> 4. Selection: **ce dont**

Je ne sais pas **ce dont** il parle.

*He doesn't speak French, **which** will be a problem.*

    1. Relative clause: which will be a problem

    2. Antecedent: "he doesn't speak French" → add **ce**   500

    3. Function of relative pronoun in French: subject

    4. Selection: **ce qui**

Il ne parle pas français, **ce qui** sera un problème.

*To speak French well, that's **what** I want.*

    1. Relative clause: what I want

    2. Antecedent: "to speak French well" → add **ce**

    3. Function of relative pronoun in French: direct object of
       vouloir *(to want)*

    4. Selection: **ce que**

Bien parler français, voilà **ce que** je veux.

CHAPTER

43

WHAT IS A DEMONSTRATIVE PRONOUN?

A **DEMONSTRATIVE PRONOUN** is a word that replaces a noun as if pointing to it. The word *demonstrative* comes from *demonstrate*, to show.

Choose a suit. *This one* is expensive. *That one* is not.

antecedent points to one suit   points to another suit

In English and French, demonstrative pronouns can be used in a variety of ways.

"THIS ONE, THAT ONE" AND "THESE, THOSE"

IN ENGLISH

The singular demonstrative pronouns are ***this (one)*** and ***that (one)***; the plural forms are ***these*** and ***those***.

Here are my suitcases. *This one* is big ; *those* are small.

antecedent singular   plural

Choose a book. *Those* are in French, *that one* is in English.

antecedent plural   singular

This (one), these refer to persons or things near the speaker, and *that (one), those* refer to persons or things further away from the speaker.

IN FRENCH

Demonstrative pronouns agree in gender with their **ANTECEDENT**; that is, the noun to which they refer. Their number depends on whether they refer to one person or thing *(this one, that one)* or to more than one person or thing *(these, those)*. Also, **-ci** is added to indicate persons or things close to the speaker and **-là** to indicate persons or things further away.

		MASCULINE	FEMININE
this, that (one)	**SINGULAR**	celui(-ci/-là)	celle(-ci/-là)
these, those	**PLURAL**	ceux(-ci/-là)	celles(-ci/-là)

To choose the correct form, follow these steps:

    1. Determine the antecedent.

    2. Determine the gender of the antecedent.

3. Number: *This one, that one* → singular; *these, those*
   → plural.
4. Based on steps 2 and 3 choose the correct form
   from the chart on p. 160.
5. Add **-ci** for *this* or *these* and **-là** for *that* and *those*.

Look at the following examples.

Which book did you read? **This one.**
   1. Antecedent: book
   2. Gender: **Livre** *(book)* is masculine.
   3. Number: This one → singular
   4. Selection: **celui**
   5. *This* → **-ci**
Quel livre as-tu lu? **Celui-ci.**

Which letter did you read? **That one.**
   1. Antecedent: letter
   2. Gender: **Lettre** *(letter)* is feminine.
   3. Number: That one → singular
   4. Selection: **celle**
   5. *That* → **-là**
Quelle lettre as-tu lue? **Celle-là.**

Which books did you read? **These.**
   1. Antecedent: books
   2. Gender: **Livres** *(books)* is masculine.
   3. Number: These → plural
   4. Selection: **ceux**
   5. *These* → **-ci**
Quels livres as-tu lus? **Ceux-ci.**

Which letters did you read? **Those.**
   1. Antecedent: letters
   2. Gender: **Lettres** *(letters)* is feminine.
   3. Number: Those → plural
   4. Selection: **celles**
   5. *Those* → **-là**
Quelles lettres as-tu lues? **Celles-là.**

TO SHOW POSSESSION: CELUI DE

IN ENGLISH

You can show possession with an apostrophe after the
possessor, without repeating the person or thing possessed mentioned in a previous sentence. The person or
thing possessed is the antecedent.

Do you have a car? No, I use my *father's.*

antecedent   possessor + apostrophe

The word *car* is not repeated after *father;* it is understood.

IN FRENCH

Remember that the apostrophe structure to show posses-sion does not exist in French (see p. 22). For the same reason that "my father's house" can only be expressed with the structure "the house *of* my father," the expres-sion "my father's" can only be expressed with a structure that does not require an apostrophe. This structure word-for-word corresponds to "the one of" (singular antecedent) or "the ones of" (plural antecedent).

Do you have a car? No, I'm using my father's.

         antecedent   possessor + apostrophe
         singular   *"the one of* my father"

Do you have your keys? No, I'm using my father's.

         antecedent   possessor + apostrophe
         plural   *"the ones of* my father"

To show possession when the person or object possessed is not stated in the same sentence, French uses the demonstrative pronouns (without **-ci** or **-là**) + **de** *(of)*.

To choose the correct form, follow these steps:

   1. Find the antecedent of *"the one"* or *"the ones."*
   2. Determine the gender and number of the antecedent.
   3. Based on step 2, select the form of the demonstra-tive pronoun (see chart p. 160).
   4. Add the preposition **de** *(of)*.

Let us apply these rules to the following examples:

Which house are you selling? ***My father's.***

    antecedent   **"*the one of* my father"**

   1. Antecedent: house
   2. Gender & number: **Maison** *(house)* is feminine singular.
   3. & 4. Selection: **celle de**

Quelle maison vendez-vous? **Celle de** mon père.

Which books are you taking? ***The young man's.***

    antecedent   **"*the ones of* the young man"**

   1. Antecedent: books
   2. Gender & number: **Livres** *(books)* is masculine plural.
   3. & 4. Selection: **ceux de**

Quels livres prenez-vous? **Ceux du** jeune homme.

"THE ONE THAT": CELUI QUI, CELUI QUE
120
(see *What is a Relative Pronoun?*, p. 147)

IN ENGLISH

The pronouns *the one* (singular antecedent) and *the ones* (plural antecedent), followed by the relative pronouns *that, which* or *who,* can start a relative clause giving us additional information about a person or thing mentioned in a previous sentence. Since the relative pronouns *that, which* or *who* are often omitted in English, we have indicated them between parentheses.

130

> What book are you reading? *The one (that)* you gave me.
>> CLAUSE: "the one that you gave me" gives us
>>> additional information about *the book*.
>> NUMBER: *The one* is singular.

> Which girls came to dinner? *The ones (that)* you invited.
>> CLAUSE: "the ones that you invited" gives us
>>> additional information about *the girls*.
>> NUMBER: *The ones* is plural.

IN FRENCH

To express the English structure above, French uses the demonstrative pronouns followed by a relative pronoun. The demonstrative pronouns agree in gender and number with the antecedent. The relative pronoun is selected according to whether it is the subject or object of the relative clause. Unlike English the relative pronoun must be stated.
140

To choose the correct form, follow these steps:

    A. Demonstrative pronoun *(the one, the ones)*
        1. Find the antecedent of *"the one"* or *"the ones."*
        2. Determine the gender and number of the antecedent.
        3. Select the French form according to the chart on p. 160.

150

    B. Relative pronoun *(that, which, who*—add to the English sentence if it has been omitted)
        1. Determine the function of the relative pronoun in the relative clause.
        2. Select the correct French form:
            ▪ subject of the relative clause → **qui**
            ▪ object of the relative clause → **que**

Let us apply these rules to the following examples:

What book are you reading? **The one (that)** *you gave me.*

    A. Demonstrative pronoun

        1. Antecedent: book

        2. Gender & number: **Livre** *(book)* is masculine singular.

        3. Selection: **celui**

    B. Relative pronoun

        1. Function: *that* is the object of the relative clause.

            (Answers the question: "You gave *what?*" *You* is the subject.)

        2. Selection: **que**

Quel livre lis-tu? **Celui que** tu m'as donné.

antecedent   dem. pronoun + relative pronoun
masc. sing.   masc. sing.   object

Which girls went to Paris? **The ones who** *spoke French.*

    A. Demonstrative pronoun

        1. Antecedent: girls

        2. Gender & number: **Filles** *(girls)* is feminine plural.

        3. Selection: **celles**

    B. Relative pronoun

        1. Function: *who* is the subject of the relative clause.

        2. Selection: **qui**

Quelles filles sont allées à Paris ? **Celles qui** parlaient français.

    antecedent   dem. pronoun + relative pronoun
    fem. pl.   fem. pl.   subject

WHAT IS MEANT BY ACTIVE
AND PASSIVE VOICE?

VOICE in the grammatical sense refers to the relationship between the verb and its subject. There are two voices, the **ACTIVE VOICE** and the **PASSIVE VOICE**.

ACTIVE VOICE — A sentence is said to be in the active voice when the subject is the performer of the action of the verb. In this instance, the verb is called an **ACTIVE VERB**.

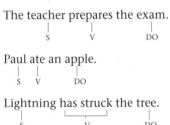

In all these examples the subject (S) performs the action of the verb (V) and the direct object (DO) is the receiver of the action (see *What is a Subject?*, p. 28 and *What are Objects?*, p. 109).

PASSIVE VOICE — A sentence is said to be in the passive voice when the subject is the receiver of the action of the verb. In this instance, the verb is called a **PASSIVE VERB**.

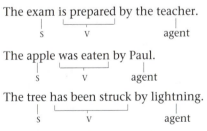

In all these examples, the subject is the receiver of the action of the verb. The performer of the action, if it is mentioned, is introduced by the word "by" and is called the **AGENT**.

IN ENGLISH

The passive voice is expressed by the verb *to be* conjugated in the appropriate tense + the past participle of the main verb (p. 59). The tense of the passive sentence is indicated by the tense of the verb *to be*.

The exam *is prepared* by the teacher.

present

The exam *was prepared* by the teacher.

past

The exam *will be prepared* by the teacher.

future

The use of the passive voice is very common in English.

IN FRENCH

As in English, a passive verb is expressed with the auxiliary **être** (*to be*) conjugated in the appropriate tense + the past participle of the main verb (pp. 59-60). The tense of the passive sentence is indicated by the tense of the verb **être**.[1]

L'examen **est** préparé par le professeur.

present

*The exam **is** prepared by the teacher.*

L'examen **a été** préparé par le professeur.

past

*The exam **has been (was)** prepared by the teacher.*

L'examen **sera** préparé par le professeur.

future

*The exam **will be** prepared by the teacher.*

Because the auxiliary in the passive voice is always **être**, the past participles in a passive sentence always agree in gender and number with the subject (see pp. 62-3).

Les vins français sont **appréciés** dans le monde entier.

subject → masc. pl.   past participle → masc. pl.

*French **wines** are **appreciated** the world over.*

---

[1]Verbs that take **être** as an auxiliary to form compound tenses in the active voice (see the list on p. 62) do not have a passive voice since they are never followed by a direct object in the active voice. For example, **aller, partir, venir**, etc. cannot be made passive.

MAKING AN ACTIVE SENTENCE PASSIVE

Verbs that form their past tenses with the auxiliary **avoir** in the active voice can become passive when the auxiliary is changed from **avoir** to **être**.

ACTIVE VERB PAST TENSE	PASSIVE VERB PRESENT TENSE
a mangé *(has eaten, ate)*	**est** mangé *(is eaten)*
a parlé *(has spoken, spoke)*	**est** parlé *(is spoken)*
a vendu *(has sold, sold)*	**est** vendu *(is sold)*

80

The steps to change an active sentence to a passive sentence are the same in English and in French.

1. The direct object of the active sentence is made the subject of the passive sentence.

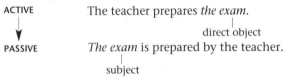

ACTIVE The teacher prepares *the exam.*
direct object

PASSIVE *The exam* is prepared by the teacher.
subject

90

2. The tense of the verb of the active sentence is reflected in the tense of the verb *to be* in the passive sentence.

ACTIVE The teacher *prepares* the exam.
present

PASSIVE The exam *is* prepared by the teacher.
present

ACTIVE The teacher *prepared* the exam.
past

PASSIVE The exam *was* prepared by the teacher.
past

100

ACTIVE The teacher *will* prepare the exam.
future

PASSIVE The exam *will be* prepared by the teacher.
future

3. The subject of the active sentence is made the agent of the passive sentence introduced with *by.*

ACTIVE *The teacher* prepares the exam.
subject

PASSIVE The exam is prepared *by the teacher.*
agent

110

The agent is often omitted.

ACTIVE   *The coach* delayed the game.

          |
          subject

↓

PASSIVE   The game was delayed *[by the coach]*.

                           |
                         agent
                         could be omitted

AVOIDING THE PASSIVE VOICE IN FRENCH

Although French has a passive voice, whenever possible French speakers try to avoid the passive construction by replacing it with an active one. There are two ways passive sentences can be avoided:

1. the **on** construction — The pronoun **on** is not only used as a replacement of the subject pronoun **nous** *(we*, see pp. 34-5). It also corresponds to the English indefinite pronoun *one,* as in the sentence, *"One* should eat when *one* is hungry." To avoid a passive construction, French often uses **on** as the subject of an active sentence when we don't know who is doing the action, even in sentences where English speakers would never use such a construction.

> *English **is spoken** in many countries.*
>> English, the subject, is not doing the speaking; therefore, the sentence is in the passive voice.
>
> **On parle** anglais dans beaucoup de pays.
>> On, the subject, is doing the speaking; therefore, the sentence is in the active voice.
>
> *The New York Times **is sold** here.*
>> The New York Times, the subject, is not doing the selling; therefore, the sentence is in the passive voice.
>
> **On vend** le New York Times ici.
>> On, the subject, is doing the selling; therefore, the sentence is in the active voice.
>
> *John **was told** that Mary speaks French.*
>> John, the subject, is not doing the telling; therefore, the sentence is in the passive voice.
>
> **On a dit** à Jean que Marie parle français.
>> On, the subject, is doing the telling; therefore, the sentence is in the active voice.

2. the reflexive verb construction — The main verb of the sentence is changed from the English passive voice to the equivalent French reflexive verb (see *What are Reflexive Pronouns and Verbs?*, p. 129). This reflexive construction is used primarily for general statements.

*English **is spoken** in many countries.*
L'anglais **se parle** dans beaucoup de pays.

160

*The New York Times **is sold** here.*
Le New York Times **se vend** ici.

CAREFUL — Verbs that form their past tenses with the auxiliary **être** in the active voice (see list p. 62) are always active; they do not have a passive voice; e.g., **il est allé** *(he went)* has no other form; it is always active. Make sure you distinguish between the auxiliary **être** + past participle used to form a present tense in the passive voice and the auxiliary **être** + past participle used to form a past tense in the active voice.

170

a, an 17-8
active voice 165
adjective 85
  adverb or adjective 102-3
  attributive 87
  comparison of 89-91
  demonstrative 85, 99-100
  descriptive 85, 86-8
  interrogative 85, 97-8
  possessive 85, 92-6
    study tips 96
  predicate 87
  study tips 88
adverb 101-3
  study tips 103
affirmative 47-8
agent 165, 167
agreement 6-7, 16
  see all headings under adjective,
    noun and article
  past participle 60, 62-3, 68,
    81, 131, 156, 166
  pronoun and antecedent *see*
    all headings under pronoun
  verb and subject 29, 35, 38-41
antecedent 30, 31, 34, 35-6, 117,
  119, 121, 125-6, 133-6, 144-5,
  147-59, 160-4
  see all headings under pronoun
any 18-9
apostrophe "s" 21-2, 161-2
article 15-9
  definite 15-7
  indefinite 17-8
  partitive 18-9
avoir (to have) 44-6, 54, 59-60,
  61-3, 67-8, 73, 81, 131, 169

be (to) 37, 166-7

ce 99, 158-9
celui 160-1
celui de 161-2
celui qui/que 163-4

clause 79, 104-5
  dependent 104-5
  if-clause 79-82
  main 104-5, 147
  relative 147-59, 163-4
  result 79-82
  subordinate 104-5, 147
cognates 3
command form (**l'impératif**) 75,
  76, 77-8
comparative 89-90, 91
conditional (**le conditionnel**) 46,
  64, 72, 76, 79-82
  as polite form 79, 80
  contrary-to-fact statement 64,
    79-82
  future-in-the-past 82
  hypothetical statement 76, 79-82
  indirect speech 82
  past (**le conditionnel passé**)
    46, 80-1, **82**
  present (**le conditionnel**
    présent) 79-80, 81, 82
conjugation 24, 37-43
  study tips 42-3
conjugation (group) 41
conjunction 104-5
  coordinating 104
  + subjunctive 84
  study tips 105
  subordinating 104-5
contraction 47, 77
contrary-to-fact statement 64, 79,
  80-1, 82

declarative sentence 50-1
direct statement 82
do/does/did
  in interrogative sentence 50
  in negative sentence 47
dont 154-6, 158

each other 131-2
en 126, 128

ending (**la terminaison**) 26, 41
être (to be) 44-6, 59-60, 61-3,
  67-8, 73, 81, 87, 131, 166, 169

familiar form **tu** 32-4, 38
feminine 9, 10-2, 16, 18-9
formal form **vous** 33-4, 38, 40
function 5, 6, 9, 23, 30, 32, 111,
  113, 114, 115, 116, 123, 139-41,
  143, 144, 148-9, 151-2, 155-7,
  158-9, 163-4
future (**le futur**) 24, 44, 53, 54,
  70-1, 72, 74, 75, 81, 82, 166-7
  immediate future (**le futur
    immédiat**) 71-2
  progressive 59
  stem 70, 80
  study tips 72
future-in-the-past 82
future perfect (**le futur antérieur**)
  46, 53, 54, 67, 73-4

gender (masculine/feminine) 10-2
  biological 11
  grammatical 11

had 46, 67
have (to) 44-6, 59, 61
he 30, 32, 37, 38, 39
him, her 30, 113, 115, 117, 119,
  120, 123-4, 125-6, 127
himself, herself 130
his, her 30, 92, 93-4, 110, 113
his, hers 133-6, 137
hypothetical statement 76, 79

I 30, 32
idiom 5
l'imparfait 54, 61, 63-4
  vs. **le passé composé** 64-5
imperative (**l'impératif**) 75, 77-8
indicative (**l'indicatif**) 53, 54, 77, 83
indirect statement 82
infinitive (**l'infinitif**) 24, 25-6, 41, 42
interrogative sentence 50-2

intransitive verb 24, 109, 110
inversion 50, 51, 140, 144
it 32, 33, 34, 37, 38, 39, 115, 117,
  119, 121, 128
its 133
itself 130, 168

lequel 144-5, 153-4, 155, 156
let's 77, 78
linking verb 87

masculine 9, 10-2, 16, 18-19
me 30, 115, 116, 118, 120, 123-5, 127
meaning 5
mine 31, 133-5, 137
mood 24, 75-6, 79, 83
my 92-4, 95, 136, 161-2
myself 30, 129-31

ne...rien/ne...personne 48-9
negative 44, 47-8, 52, 77-8
negative words 48-9
neuter 9, 10, 11, 92, 133
not 47-8, 77-8, 89-90
noun (common/proper) 8-9, 10, 39
  agreement with article 15-9
  collective 13
  compound 8
  count/non-count 18-9
  study tips 20
number (singular/plural) 9, 13-4

object 23, 109-14
  direct 30, 63, 109-10, 114
  English vs. French 112-3
  indirect 30, 110-1, 114
  object of a preposition 112, 114
  sentences w/direct and indirect
    object 111-2
on 32, 34-5, 40
  to avoid passive 168
one (the), the ones (that) 163-4
our 85, 92, 94-5
ours 133, 136-7
ourselves 30, 129, 130

participle (**le participe**) 24, 58-60
  past (**le participe passé**) 45, 46
    54, 59-60, 61-3, 67, 73, 80-1,
    131, 156, 166
  present (**le participe présent**)
    58-9
parts of speech 5-6
le passé composé (present perfect)
  45-6, 53, 54, 61-3
  vs. **l'imparfait** 64-5
  study tips 65-6
passive voice 24, 28, 109, 165-9
  avoiding in French 167-9
  present passive vs. **passé composé**
    168-9
past perfect (**le plus-que-parfait**)
  46, 53, 54, 67-9, 73, 80-1
past tense (**le passé**) 54, 61-6, 75,
  79, 83, 169
  see **l'imparfait** *and* **le passé**
    composé
  past emphatic 53, 61
  past progressive 53, 58-9, 61, 64,
    67, 68
  simple past 61, 67, 68, 81, 83
person (grammatical) 32
pluperfect *see* past perfect
plural 13-4
le plus-que-parfait *see* past perfect
polite form 32
possessive 21-2
preposition 106-7
  to change meaning of verb 26
  dangling 141-2
  prepositional phrase 106
  study tips 107-8
present perfect (**le passé composé**)
  45-6, 53, 54, 61-3
present tense (**le présent**) 24, 37,
  44, 45, 53-4, 56-7, 68, 71, 74, 78
  present emphatic 53, 56
  present progressive 53, 56, 59, 71
pronoun 30-1

demonstrative 31
disjunctive (**le pronoun personnel**
  tonique) 30, 123-8
indefinite 31
interrogative 31, 98, 139-46
  as direct object 140-1, 143-4
  as indirect object 141-3, 144
  as object of preposition 141-4
  as subject 31, 139-40, 143-4
  study tips 146
object 115-22
  direct 30, 115-7, 120-1
  indirect 30, 115, 118-9, 120-1
  of preposition 123, 124-6,
    127-8
  study tips 122
  summary object pronouns
    120-1
  summary object and disjunctive
    pronouns 127-8
personal 30
subject 30, 32-6
  study tips 36
possessive 31, 133-8
  study tips 137-8
reflexive 30
relative 31, 147-59
  direct object 150
  indirect object/object of
    preposition 151-4
  object of preposition **de** 154-5
  object of prepositions other
    than **de** 153-4
  omission 150-1, 152-3
  subject 148-9
  without antecedent 157-9
reciprocal action 131-2

sentence 23
  affirmative 47-8
  complete 23
  declarative 50-1
  interrogative 50-1
  negative 44, 47-8

shall 70
she 32, 37, 38, 39
si-clause 80, 81-2
singular 13
some 18-9
stem (**la racine**) 41
subject 28-9
subjunctive 76, 83-4, 105
superlative 90-1

tag question 52
tense 24, 44
  compound tense 45
  simple tense 45, 53-5
  study tips 54-5
that 99-100, 148-9, 150-1, 155-5
that (this) one 160-1
the 15-6
their 92, 94-5
theirs 133, 135-6
them 115, 117, 119, 121, 123-6
themselves 129, 132
these, those 99-100, 160-1
they 32-3, 35-6
this 99-100
transitive verb 24, 109-10
tu familiar form 32-34, 38

us 115, 116-7, 118, 123, 124-5
used to 61, 64

verb 23-4
  active/passive 165
  auxiliary verb (helping verb) 44-6,
    50, 52, 53, 54, 58-60, 61-3, 67-8,
    70, 73, 131, 166, 169
    see also **avoir** *and* être
  conjugation 37-43
  ending 25, 41
  helping 44-6
  intransitive 24 109, 110
  irregular 37-8, 41, 42
  linking 87
  looking up in dictionary 26
  main 45-7

reciprocal 131-2 .
reflexive 27, 129-32
  to avoid passive 168-9
regular 37-8, 41-2
stem 41
study tips 27
transitive 24, 109, 110
vocabulary 1-2
voice (active/passive) 24, 28, 165-9
vous formal form 33, 95

we 32-3, 37-8, 40
what 97-8, 139-44, 157-9
which 85, 97-8, 148-9, 150, 153-8
which one (ones) 144-5
who 139-44, 147-9, 155, 163
whom 140-3, 150-5, 157
whose 31, 155
will 70
will have 73
would 64
  see also conditional present
would have 80-2
  see also conditional past

y 119
you 32-4, 37-8, 40, 78, 95, 115-6,
  118, 120, 125-6, 127, 129
your 92-5
yours 133-7
yourself, yourselves 129-31